2495
Mil

STEEL SHARK

IN THE

PACIFIC

USS PAMPANITO

SS-383

STEEL SHARK

IN THE
PACIFIC

USS PAMPANITO
SS-383

by
Capt. Walter W. Jaffee

THE GLENCANNON PRESS

MARITIME BOOKS

PALO ALTO
2001

This book is Copyright © 2001
Published by The Glencannon Press
P.O. Box 341, Palo Alto, CA 94302
Tel. 800-711-8985
www.glencannon.com

First Edition, first printing.

Library of Congress Cataloging-in-Publication Data

Jaffee, Walter W.
    Steel shark in the Pacific : USS Pampanito SS-383 / by Walter W.
Jaffee.-- 1st ed.
      p. cm.
    Includes biliographical references and index.
    ISBN 1-889901-16-4 (alk. paper)
    1. Pampanito (Sumarine) 2. World War, 1939-1945--Naval Operations,
American. 3. World War, 1939-1945--Campaigns--Pacific Ocean. 4.
World War, 1939-1945--Naval operations--Sumarine. I. Title

D774.P34 J34 2001
940.54'51--dc21

                                      00-064685

To Russell Booth
whose passion was USS *Pampanito,*
to those who sailed her,
and
to the men and women of
the San Francisco Maritime National Park Association
who keep her alive
and preserve her history for all to remember.

By the same author:

The Last Mission Tanker, Mission Santa Ynez
The Lane Victory, *a Victory Ship in War and in Peace*
The Last Liberty, the Biography of the SS Jeremiah O'Brien
Appointment in Normandy, the Jeremiah O'Brien*'s Return For
       the 50th Anniversary of D-Day in 1994*
The Track of the Golden Bear, *the Training Ships of California
       Maritime Academy*
The Presidential Yacht Potomac, the history of Franklin D.
       Roosevelt's "Floating White House."
*Heritage of the Sea, The Training Ships of Maine Maritime
       Academy*

He goes a great voyage that goes to the bottom of the sea.

George Herbert

Like the destroyer, the submarine has created its own type of officer and man — with language and traditions apart from the rest of the Service, and yet at heart unchangingly of the Service.

Rudyard Kipling

ACKNOWLEDGMENTS

Many people were a great help in this writing of the *Pampanito* story. It certainly could not have been done without the cooperation of the San Francisco Maritime National Park Association and the staff and crew of the submarine itself. In particular, Chris Bach, *Pampanito* manager, and Tom Richardson, assistant manager, kindly pointed me in the right direction and gave me access to the boat's files and records. The Association's efficient organization of materials made a daunting job far less so.

I'd like to thank all those who made time in their busy schedules to be interviewed: Chris Bach, Bill Fisk, Al MacDonald, Charles McGuire, Tom Richardson, Bob Taylor and Marvin Wong. In addition, many of the former crew filled out questionnaires and corresponded: Louis Bobb, Harry Bowring, Robert Bennett, Clarence Carmody, Robert Diltz, Jack Evans, Cliff Grommett, Ona Hawkins, Gordon Hopper, Frank Lederer, Michael Manning, Elmer Smith, Jacob Stappler, Spencer Stimler, Albert Van Atta, Roger Walters, Earl Watkins, Woodrow Weaver and Clarence Williams. A major part of the story comes from them.

A special thanks to Tom Richardson for reviewing the rough manuscript. His many years of involvement with *Pampanito* and his vast knowledge of its restoration history have been a valuable resource.

Finally, I'd like to thank my publisher for her support, her skill with the written word and her perseverance in keeping me on track.

Contents

INTRODUCTION

The maritime industry is a small fraternity. You meet people during one phase of your life, then find your paths crossing and recrossing through the years. So it was with Russell Booth, to whom this book is dedicated, and the person who, more than anyone, made the USS *Pampanito* a crown jewel of the historic ships on the San Francisco waterfront.

We first met when I was superintendent of the Suisun Bay Reserve Fleet, an agency of the Maritime Administration. He came looking for parts and equipment to help restore the boat. Because of a little known government process that allows for the transfer of equipment from one agency to another, and because *Pampanito* was affiliated with the National Park Service (a government agency), we were able to let him take what he needed. Encouraged, he came back several times.

Sometime later, there was a reception at the Maritime Museum for the former crew of USS *Pampanito* and a number of former POWs from Australia. We were a diverse group — veterans, POWs, preservationists, volunteers, friends in the maritime community. The submarine was a common bond. But that bond was strongest between the former crew and the POWs: the boat had been the setting for their great World War II adventure — their home, their life and, for some, their salvation.

After I left the Reserve Fleet, Russell and I ran into each other at museum functions and there was always time for a few words about the boat, how the restoration was going and what each of us was doing with our lives. Sadly, Russell passed away, much too soon, but he left the *Pampanito* in capable hands.

While researching the boat's archives for this book, I met two more people from the past. Tom Richardson, now assistant manager for *Pampanito*, recalled coming to the Reserve Fleet on those "shopping trips" and Chris Bach, manager of the project, was in a class I taught at California Maritime Academy some years ago — again, paths crossing and recrossing.

USS *Pampanito* touched a lot of our lives. Hers is a story that needs to be told. That she can be seen and visited and appreciated by millions today is a tribute to everyone involved.

I sincerely wish Russell Booth could be here to share in this book. His passion for saving ships and his enthusiasm were infectious. He would have been a constant inspiration — no, he is still a constant inspiration.

My own passion is for preserving ships through the written word. I hope I have done him and the boat justice.

Capt. Walter W. Jaffee
Menlo Park, California
August 2000

1

THE
FLEET
SUBMARINE

P owerful. Formidable. Sinister. The United States Navy fleet
submarine in World War II was a near perfect blend of
function, form and design. Later boats are faster — both
above and below the surface. They carry more accurate
torpedoes, missiles and listening devices, navigate with
ultimate precision and house larger crews in greater comfort. But modern
boats have lost that character that made the boats of World War II's
"Silent Service" so distinctive — the virtue of looking like what they
were — powerful and formidable engines of war.

The U.S. Navy's fleet submarine was the result of a natural
evolution in the shipcrafter's, or, more accurately, the submersible-
crafter's, art and the role of the vessel which began in World War I. The
early problems of reliable propulsion and weaponry had been solved by
diesel engines and batteries and by the torpedo. By 1914 almost every
country in the world had a submarine fleet — Austria, six boats; France,
forty-five boats; Germany, twenty-nine boats, Great Britain, seventy-

seven boats; Italy, eighteen boats; Denmark, seven boats; Greece, two boats; The Netherlands, seven boats; Japan, thirteen boats; Norway, four boats; Peru, two boats; Portugal, one boat; Russia, twenty-eight boats; Sweden five boats and the United States, thirty-five boats. But because it was a new vehicle to warfare, its purpose and use were tentative.

Most countries, particularly in Europe, built their submarines for coastal defense. Until 1914 each side merely used its submarines for patrol. The Germans set up a defense line against the anticipated invasion by Britain. British submarines watched the movements of surface ships. The first casualties were two German U-boats. The *U-15* was cut in half on August 9, 1914 by the British cruiser HMS *Birmingham* and the *U-13* was sunk by a mine. The British view was that perhaps submarines weren't much to be concerned about after all.

That quickly changed on September 22, 1914 when the *U-9,* under Kapitän-leutnant Otto Weddigen sank three 12,000-ton armored British cruisers in just over one hour. HMS *Aboukir,* HMS *Cressy* and HMS *Hogue* took more than 1,400 men to the bottom. Suddenly, the submarine was a very serious consideration, indeed. And a deadly, new role for the submarine quickly became apparent: it could be used to attack and sink ships of the enemy's battle line.

The British response was to provide destroyer escorts for all its larger ships. Destroyers of the time had no special weapons to counteract the submarine menace, but they were fast, maneuverable and a difficult target. Standard practice was to fight off U-boats with deck guns or ram them. In fact, new British destroyers were built with a strengthened forefoot on their bows for this purpose. All such countermeasures

> **WHEN IS A SUBMARINE NOT A SUBMARINE?**
>
> Technically, a submersible vessel is one designed for surface operations but which has the ability to submerge for short periods of time. A true submarine is designed specifically to cruise underwater. Only nuclear powered submarines, with their unlimited fuel supply which gives them the ability to stay submerged for months, are true submarines. However, common usage refers to all underwater warships as submarines.

Submarines are called "boats" because originally they were very similar in design and use to torpedo boats. That slang term stayed with them. They are never referred to as ships.

depended on the destroyer's crew visually sighting the undersea boat, something submarine commanders naturally guarded against.

At the outbreak of World War I, all belligerent and neutral countries subscribed to the precepts of International Law and the Hague Convention for the conduct of war at sea: no warship (which now included submarines) was allowed to fire on a merchant ship that was not carrying offensive weapons and not acting in a hostile manner. According to the Prize Regulations, it was understood that the submarine or warship would stop the merchantman, examine her papers, identify herself and then sink the victim or sail her home with a prize crew. This created serious problems for submarines. To comply, they would have to surface and in so doing lose their stealth and effectiveness. In addition, submarines carried too few men to send off prize crews on every ship they captured. The first, and almost the last, time a German U-boat complied with such requirements was when the *U-17* stopped the steamer *Glitra* off Norway on October 20, 1914. Rather than provide a prize crew, the steamer was scuttled. She was the first victim in the submarine war on trade. Soon, U-boats began attacking merchant shipping with impunity. With warships constantly protected by their destroyer screens, the lone merchantmen were much easier prey.

Germany now realized a second, and possibly more important use for the submarine — as an offensive weapon to cut off her enemy's supply lines. By February 4, 1915 she had declared the waters around Britain a War Zone and warned that any British or French ships entering the area would be sunk. It was also declared that it would "not always be possible" to prevent attacks on neutral shipping. Losses quickly mounted, from 47,900 tons in January to 185,800 tons in August, the most notable being the *Lusitania* on May 7, 1915 sunk with the loss of 1,201 lives.

Under the threat of United States intervention Germany went back to the Prize Regulations. But with the indecisive Battle of Jutland in May of 1916, the continued blockade of Germany by Britain, and a U-Boat Fleet now numbering 105, Germany finally abandoned them completely, declaring unrestricted submarine warfare on February 1, 1917. Her intent was to reduce Britain's supply lines to the point that she

The term U-boat comes from the German word for submarine, *unterseeboot, which translates as "under sea boat."*

could not continue the war on the continent and to do so before the United States had time to react.

Germany now dominated the oceans around Great Britain, in the Mediterranean and in Russia's far north. In February, 254 ships were sunk. U-boats accounted for 310 vessels in March and 413 in April. U-boat losses amounted to a mere nine vessels. German submarines crossed the Atlantic, disrupting coastal shipping in America. *U-151*, under Lieutenant Commander Heinrich von Nostitz und Janckendorff, led the way in 1918. Laying mines off Baltimore and Delaware, he attacked three fishing schooners, cut two underwater cables and sank six ships off New Jersey. On June 2, 1918 he attacked the passenger ship *Carolina*. By the time she headed for home, *U-151* had twenty-seven ships to her credit, four by mines. Janckendorff's cruise was a bitter foreshadowing of events to come in the next war.

Germany's command of the underseas was short-lived. The offensive use of U-boats quite naturally brought retaliation from her

After forty-eight hours in a lifeboat, these survivors of the steamer Carolina *gathered in Atlantic City, New Jersey to pose in borrowed clothing. National Archives.*

enemies. In 1916 the British began using depth charges. Aircraft were a tremendous deterrent, their presence forcing U-boats beneath the surface thereby limiting them to slow speeds and greatly reducing their range. Most effective of all was the convoy, an old tactic, but one that made submarine attack especially difficult. Convoys brought merchant ships under the protection of war ships, which were what the U-boats had been avoiding by attacking lone merchant ships. Wireless telegraphy improved intership communication and careful planning relieved port congestion and limited shipments to essentials, thus reducing the number of ships available to be sunk. In the end, defensive measures countered, then eliminated, the U-boats' effectiveness.

But, in reviewing events at the end of the war, world powers recognized that the submarine had surfaced as a major weapon in naval warfare. Britain lost more than nine million tons of merchant shipping, about ninety percent of the ships registered under the British flag in 1914. All other countries, combined, lost about four million tons. Included in these figures were ten capital ships, eighteen cruisers, 5,078 merchant ships and more than 15,000 merchant seamen and civilians. During the height of Germany's unrestricted submarine warfare, the undersea boat had all but shut down the coastal waters of the Atlantic Ocean, the Mediterranean, the Baltic and the Black Sea. To military minds, this was a lesson well worth remembering.

When the Armistice between Germany and the Allies was signed on November 11, 1918, one of the key provisions included the surrender of U-boats. The victors wanted to study the sinister new weapon that produced such a devastating effect on their fleets. A total of 176 boats were turned in: 105 went to Great Britain, forty-six to France, ten to Italy, seven to Japan, six to the United States and two to Belgium. It is noteworthy that both Japan and the United States chose the larger, longer range "U-cruiser" type submarine for their share of the surrendered tonnage.

The American fleet submarine of World War II can trace its lineage directly to the German U-boats taken for study at the end of World War I. Plagued by mechanical breakdowns, low endurance and poor seakeeping, the U.S. Navy's World War I submarine fleet was badly in

German U-boats, reparations from World War I, under study at the Brooklyn Navy Yard in April 1919. UPI/Corliss-Bettman.

need of improvement. Those that looked into the future saw Japan as the most likely enemy in any coming war. The American submarine of the 1920s was therefore designed with the Pacific Ocean as its potential battle field. Two basic types of vessel were envisioned. One, a small, coastal submarine, was intended to protect important shorelines and island possessions. Such areas included the Panama Canal, Hawaii, Guam and the Philippines. The second type was the fleet submarine. A larger boat, it was designed to accompany the battle fleet, gather intelligence about enemy vessel movements and make preemptive strikes at enemy warships before major sea battles of surface ships. Because of the vast distances in the Pacific, this meant developing a boat with a long cruising range and long endurance. The boats would also have to be comfortably habitable, highly reliable and have a large capacity for torpedoes.

The hull form of the *Argonaut*, launched in 1927, was based directly on German practice and the Cachelot-class, launched in 1933, was modeled on the *U-135*. The high endurance and heavy torpedo armament of the *U-140*, a 302 foot vessel that carried two 5.9-inch guns,

USS Nautilus *(SS-168) copied many of the characteristics of Germany's U-117 and U-142 from World War I. Armed with 6-inch guns she was launched in 1930 and served in the Pacific throughout World War II.* Sea Power, A Modern Illustrated Military History.

were incorporated into the Barracuda- and Narwhal-classes (the *Narwhal* and *Nautilus* each carried two six-inch guns). Eventually, the fleet submarine evolved through changes in size, propulsion, ballast, compartmentation and torpedo tube capacity from the Tambor-class to the Gato-, Balao- and Tench classes. Here the American World War II submarine reached its zenith.

The 5-inch/25 was the most popular gun carried on fleet submarines during World War II. Sea Power.

The differences between the three boats were minor. Basically, they displaced 1,810 tons on the surface or 2,410 submerged. Measuring

The U.S. Navy fleet submarine reached its development peak in the Gato-, Balao- and Tench-classes. Pampanito *was in the Balao class.*

just under 312 feet in length with a beam of 27 feet 3 inches, they had a draft of 15 feet 3 inches. Their twin propellers were driven by electric motors with two sources of power: diesel generator sets on the surface or batteries when submerged. The diesel-electric drive achieved 5,400 shaft horsepower and the batteries 2,740 shaft horsepower. Armament included six bow and four stern torpedo tubes while the deck armament varied from sub to sub according to how new the boat was, its last major yard period and preferences of the boat's commanding officer. Variations included either a 3-inch/50, 4-inch/50 or 5-inch/25 for the main gun and combinations of 40mm Bofors and 20mm Oerlikon aintiaircraft guns and portable .30 cal. and .50 cal. machine guns. The sub's typical wartime complement was eighty (seventy enlisted men and ten officers).

The fleet submarine was a compact and complicated fighting machine. In a space the size of the average six-room house were as many compartments as a warship three times the boat's size. In addition to

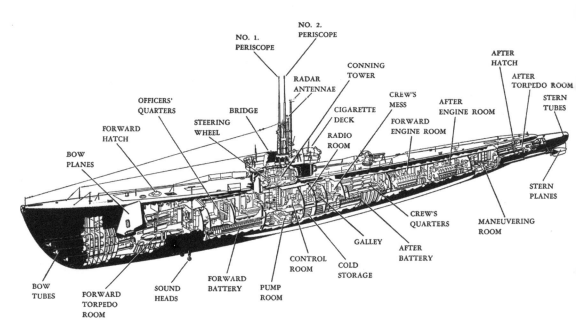

The typical fleet submarine was a formidable fighting machine and a home to her officers and crew. U.S. Navy

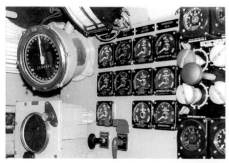

A small fraction of the complex instrumentation and controls of a fleet submarine is shown by, clockwise from left, distiller, No. 4 diesel engine instrument panel, No. 4 generator instrument panel, No. 3 generator instrument panel, depth gauge, main propulsion control stand and torpedo tube blow controls. Author

living accommodations for her crew of eighty, the fleet submarine contained a control room, diesel engines, electric motors, water tanks, fuel tanks and 252 battery cells, each weighing more than one ton. There were air compressors and high-pressure air banks for blowing tanks and charging torpedo air flasks. The torpedo rooms held ten torpedo tubes and storage space for twenty-four torpedoes. Elsewhere were refrigerated and dry store spaces, stills for making fresh water, air-conditioning and air-purifying systems, ice machines, showers, main ballast tanks to provide positive buoyancy when surfaced and neutral buoyancy when submerged, variable tanks for adjusting trim, electrical and hydraulic equipment for operating the bow and stern planes, wells for the periscopes, a lazaret, chain locker, ammunition magazines, galley, navigation instruments, fire control instruments, radio, radar, sonar, valves, gauges, meters, operating levers, oil lines, water lines, air lines and electrical cables. And all contained inside a hull capable of withstanding pressures hundreds of feet below the surface.

The fleet submarine's crew was an equally complicated mix of cross-trained specialists. Fewer than twenty percent of the men were non-rated. Each man was required to know not only his own job but that of his shipmates, as well. The electrician's mate had to know how to fire the torpedoes, the torpedoman's mate had to understand charging the batteries. Numerically, most of the crew was made up of motor machinist's mates (called "motor macs"), electrician's mates and torpedoman's mates. The next largest group operated the radio equipment and electronic gear. Completing the complement were three quartermasters or signalmen, two ship's cooks, two steward's mates, one pharmacist's mate, one gunner's mate, one yeoman and several firemen and seamen.

The senior officer or captain was typically a Lt. Cdr. in his mid-thirties. Directly under him was the executive officer who, in addition to being second in command, served as navigator. Other officers included the chief engineer, torpedo and gunnery officer, communications officer, commissary officer and radar officer. Officers were frequently assigned more than one of these duties. Early in the war, a fleet submarine's complement was five officers and fifty-four men, but by war's end, with improvements in fire control, radar, radio and sound equipment, the complement was eight officers and seventy-five enlisted men.

Watch-standing was divided into three sections with each section standing four hours on duty and eight hours off duty. The captain stood no watch but was always on call. Each watch section was organized to man the necessary stations for diving, surfacing and surfaced or submerged cruising. Torpedo attacks and gun attacks required all hands. The captain took over the periscope and guided the approach and attack. The exec backed up the captain, double-checking his observations and calculations. Other officers served as the diving officer, torpedo data computer operator and plotting officer. In addition, one officer was usually assigned to each torpedo room to supervise readying the tubes and reloading them. Enlisted men manned the approach and fire control parties, served as telephone talkers, timekeepers or recorders. Torpedoman's mates ran their assigned torpedo rooms with any not having specific duties elsewhere required to assist with reloading.

The ninety-ninth boat in the Balao-class was USS *Pampanito,* SS-383.[1]

---

1 *Conway's All The World's Fighting Ships 1922-1946* lists *Pampanito* as No. 99 in her class, however, some boats were built out of sequence and other contracts were cancelled making her technically the 85th boat in her class.

2

USS *Pampanito*
(SS-383)

*P*ampanito was built at the Portsmouth Naval Shipyard in Portsmouth, New Hampshire. Located near Kittery, Maine, the Portsmouth shipyard rests on Seavey Island in the Piscataqua River, at the boundary between Maine and New Hampshire.

Naval shipbuilding at Portsmouth is part of a tradition of Yankee ingenuity and craftsmanship that goes back to the beginning of our nation and includes several "firsts." Among them Portsmouth claims:

- the first warship built in North America, HMS *Falkland,* in 1690.
- the heaviest ship ever laid down in North America at the time, *America,* launched in 1782.
- the first U.S. Navy shipyard to be established, in 1800.
- the first submarine built in a U.S. Naval Shipyard, *L-8* in 1917.
- the first U.S. submarine built with all-welded steel hull, USS *Snapper* in 1937.

When World War I broke out, submarine construction in the United States was a monopoly in the hands of two private companies: Electric Boat Co. and Lake Torpedo Boat Co. Each change in design brought about an increase in contract price and construction costs soared. It was decided to plan and build a submarine in a Navy yard where testing, experimentation and design changes could take place under Navy, rather than civilian, supervision. The Portsmouth Yard was selected and the keel of *L-8* was laid in late 1914. She was completed three years later at a cost well below her contract price. Thus began a long line of Portsmouth-built submarines.

Interest in submarines increased as the United States entered the war and six more submarine keels were laid between March 26, 1917 and October 10, 1918. Even after the war ended, Portsmouth continued as the Navy's premier builder of submarines on the Atlantic coast, with six S boats being completed by 1923. Five Fleet type V class submarines were built between 1923 and 1929 and were still in service in 1945.

The Depression years had a predictable effect on the yard, with only eight submarines being completed between 1930 and 1937.

In the years immediately preceding World War II the yard built approximately two fleet- type submarines each year, bringing the total to thirty-three for the period 1917 to 1941. The yard's Design Division became one of the leaders in submarine design and about half the boats that took part in World War II were designed by Portsmouth. The all-

> **SUBMARINE NAMES**
>
> At first, the U.S. Navy named its submarines with a letter according to their class and a number indicating the particular boat. Thus, during World War I, boats were A- through T-class. In addition, each boat was given an identification number, for instance the submarine named N-4 (fourth boat in the N-class) was also number SS-56. In 1931, with the development of the V-class, boats were named after marine creatures and *Barracuda,* also named *V-1,* became the first boat of the Barracuda-class. In 1939 the practice of naming submarines by class letter and number was abandoned when all submarines were assigned SS hull numbers. Henceforth, each was named after a marine creature and the first boat of a class gave its name to that class. Thus *Pampanito* SS-383 was a Balao-class boat.

The SS prefix used in submarine numbers is simply a U.S. Navy classification meaning submarine. It is not, as some might think, the first two letters of "Submersible Ship" or any other phrase.

welded USS *Snapper*, commissioned on December 15, 1937 is noteworthy because the stronger hull construction allowed the boat to submerge deeper and better withstand depth charge attacks.

Entry into World War II created a tremendous boost in Portsmouth's building program and by December 1943, contracts existed for 104 submarines. Thirty-two submarines were completed in 1944 with four being launched on the same day, January 27, 1944. Building time was reduced from 469 days per boat in 1941 to 173 days in 1944. The work force at Portsmouth reached a peak of 20,466 men and women in December 1943.

The first hull sections for USS *Picuda* (SS-382) and USS *Pampanito* (SS-383) were placed in Portsmouth's newly-constructed submarine basin on March 15, 1943. Traditionally, this is referred to as the "keel laying" but, in reality, two prefabricated hull sections were lowered in place by the yard's cranes. SS-382 and SS-383 were the first two of ten subs to be constructed in the basin. Later, to meet the increased demands of the war, submarines were assembled in the dry docks which were normally used to repair vessels. *Pampanito* (*continued on page 19*)

The first hull sections for Picuda *(SS-382) and* Pampanito *(SS-383) are lowered into place on March 15, 1943. Portsmouth Naval Shipyard.*

Mrs. James Wolfenden, above, left, was Pampanito's *sponsor. She is accompanied by Rear Admiral and Mrs. Thomas Withers. The tag on the left is believed to have been issued as an admittance badge, allowing the wearer to witness the launching. San Francisco Maritime National Park Association.*

The moment of impact, above, as the champagne splatters across the bow of Pampanito. *The First-Day-Of-Issue cover, below, reproduced the front of the launching program on an envelope with the issuance of a new stamp. San Francisco Maritime National Park Association.*

WHAT IS A PAMPANITO?

A perch-like fish of the family *carangidae,* the pampanito is found in the ocean waters off the southeast coast of China, the Dutch East Indies and the northeast coast of Australia. It feeds on slow-moving crustaceans, small crabs and small fish. Considered an excellent food fish, it is marketed fresh or dried and salted. By coincidence, these same waters are where USS *Pampanito* spent much of her time on war patrol. Courtesy FishBase WWW:Taxonomy

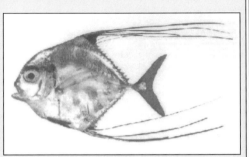

Capt. C.H. Roper, USN, reads the commissioning orders aboard Pampanito *on November 6, 1943, the date the boat officially became part of the U.S. Navy. San Francisco Maritime National Park Association.*

Rear Admiral Thomas Withers, USN, addressing Pampanito's *officers and crew at her commissioning. San Francisco Maritime National Park Association.*

(*continued from page 15*) and *Picuda* were launched on July 12 in a double ceremony honoring the first two boats to be floated out of the new construction basin. Mrs. James Wolfenden sponsored the boat. Following launching, work continued fitting her out and on November 6, 1943 *Pampanito* was commissioned an official part of the U.S. Fleet.

The new boat's crew came from all walks of life. Some left college, others gave up their jobs, many lied about their age to join the Navy and do their part for the war effort. It is difficult from the distance of half a century to put into perspective the sense of urgency that existed toward protecting our way of life. The United States was embroiled in a battle against two sinister and capable enemies: Germany and Japan. The threat was very real. If either of these were successful, Americans would lose their freedoms — of speech, of thought, of free will. The democratic ideals of the founding fathers would be ground under the jack-booted heel of totalitarianism. Ignited by Pearl Harbor, a sense of patriotism burned

throughout the land. From the youngest to the oldest, everyone knew we were fighting not only for our lives but for our way of life, our ideals and our dignity. Those had to be preserved at all costs.

Patriotic fervor was ignited by posters similar to one the above. U.S. Navy

Earl F. Watkins, motor machinist's mate 2/c: "I was very proud to be in the submarine service. I felt it was my duty. You did what you had to for your country."

Harry Bowring, motor machinist mate 2/c: "I felt an urgency to fight for my country. I didn't want to see Old Glory go down."

Posters such as this encouraged Pampanito *crewmembers to join the Navy. U.S. Navy*

Gordon Hopper, seaman 1/c: "I left college in my senior year to enlist in the U.S. Naval Reserve because I believed it was the thing to do."

Spencer Stimler, radio technician 2/c: "I was gung ho to avenge Pearl Harbor. We were all patriotic and proud of our country and ready to protect it."

Clarence Williams, electrician's mate 2/c: "Everyone was doing it. I joined the Navy at seventeen years old."

Elmer Smith, torpedoman 2/c: "I was proud to be a submariner and fighting the war."

"I felt an urgency to fight for my country. I didn't want to see Old Glory go down." Harry Bowring

Robert Bennett, torpedoman 1/c: "I wanted to do my duty."

For the officers, most of whom were career Navy men, submarine service was a fast track to advancement. Responsibility and command came much earlier in submarines than with the surface fleet.

After commissioning, *Pampanito's* crew spent from November 29 to January 15, 1944 conducting sea trials and training exercises in the icy waters off Portsmouth and New London, Connecticut. This was the time to be sure that everything operated the way it should, from main engines to galley stove to diving planes to torpedo tubes. Crash dives, emergency full astern, rapid surfacing were the order of the day as the boat was put through every conceivable maneuver. Practice attack approaches were made and exercise torpedoes were fired. All of the deck guns were fired and equipment was calibrated. This was also the first chance for the crew to begin working together, learning each other's characteristics and work habits.

In a submarine, more than in any other vessel, each member of the crew was vital. A mistake by any one person could lead to disaster. There was a special camaraderie and informality in the cramped, cheek-to-jowl existence on board. A different kind of discipline existed, maintained more by competence and self-respect than rank. Eventually, the crew would become bonded by the shared trials, miseries, unique hazards and their own proficiency in overcoming them.

One sea trial was a six day practice war patrol, conducted to get the men acquainted with the boat and what was expected of each of them. During this patrol a problem developed with the propeller shaft bearings. Made of the hard wood, lignum vitae, they wouldn't seat properly and eleven days were needed in drydock adjusting them. They would require more attention once the boat got to Hawaii.

The New England winter made the training exercises a bitter experience. William Grady, motor machinist's mate: "We had our shakedown cruise off the coast of Portsmouth, New Hampshire. We got all these heavy sheepskin coats. The new mooring lines would freeze and they'd throw them down in the forward torpedo hatch and have them on deck. I thought it was more uncomfortable and unhappy operating there than anywhere."

Robert Bennett: "I used to be on anchor detail. I was the first guy on the deck coming into port and the last guy to go down when we left.

Every night, two or three times during the night we'd drag the anchor, the ship would get close to the shore, we had to go up there with the flashlight, looking over at that anchor. Pick the anchor up and move the ship. Two or three times stealing my precious sleep."

Although many of the crew were new to *Pampanito,* there were experienced submariners aboard to train and qualify the new hands. Commanding Officer Lt. Cdr. Charles Jackson, Jr. came from the USS *Spearfish* (SS-190), and Executive Officer Paul E. Summers had been assigned to *Pampanito* following seven war patrols on the USS *Stingray* (SS-186). Others came fresh out of submarine school. Woodrow Weaver, torpedoman 1/c, volunteered because of the pay: "It was announced the submarine force was seeking volunteers. They made fifty per cent more pay as compensation for hazardous duty. I immediately volunteered.

"After a physical exam I was accepted and on completion of the torpedo course was ordered to New London, Connecticut for submarine school.

"The submarine school lasted about eight weeks. We were trained on the old 'O' and 'R' boats constructed during World War I and in the early 1920s. These old subs were so different from the fleet type subs we were to serve on, about the only thing we learned was the basics of submarine operation.

"I was advanced to torpedoman first class in August of 1943. On completion of the submarine school, I was assigned as part of the commissioning crew of the USS *Pampanito* (SS-383). The *Pampanito* was under construction at the Portsmouth Navy Yard in Portsmouth, New Hampshire. I reported around the middle of September.

"The *Pampanito* was scheduled for completion and commissioning around the first of November. The weeks in between were taken up with checking equipment and attending classes on the submarine. The new submarine recruits were expected to qualify as soon as possible. Only qualified submariners (those that knew the sub inside out) were allowed to wear the coveted 'dolphins,' the insignia of a submariner. It took me about three months to qualify."

On January 15, 1944 *Pampanito* left New London bound for the Pacific. Sailing south she went through the Panama Canal on January 24. It was the first transit of the Canal for many of the crew and interest was

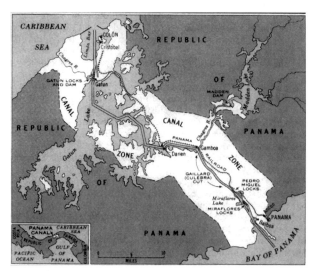

The Panama Canal, crossroads of the world. Balboa is on the Pacific side at the lower right. Encyclopedia Britannica.

high. The heat and humidity of Panama were a pleasant change from the cold waters and icy winds off Portsmouth.

As the pilot boarded and the boat eased her way toward the first set of locks, most of the crew were on deck. Tufts of white clouds occasionally gathered in the sky, creating sudden downpours that passed as quickly as they formed. In Gatun Locks they watched as their boat rose to the level of the lake beyond. Then it was across Gatun Lake whose small, jungle covered islands were home to hundreds of brightly colored birds calling back and forth. Here and there were crocodiles, sunning on a mud beach

Miraflores locks as seen from the Pacific approach with Miraflores lake beyond and Pedro Miguel Locks in the distance. Panama Canal Company

or lazily fish-tailing out of the *Pampanito*'s way. Soon the passage narrowed and they were in Gaillard Cut. Now, the banks of the Canal towered above them, the broad scars left by the excavators' steam shovels decades earlier forming still-visible steps from bottom to top.

At the Pacific end were two sets of locks, Pedro Miguel and Miraflores. Passing through them lowered the boat to the level of that ocean and soon they were tying up to one of the docks in Balboa.

Pampanito spent four days in Balboa for minor repairs and tests. It was the crew's first foreign port and a chance to let loose after the constant tension of weeks of trials, tests and drills.

Some of the crew were just recovering from seasickness. Duncan Brown, seaman 2/c: "I got seasick. I lay between the port two torpedoes in the forward torpedo room. I laid there for three days and all we did was roll from one side to the other. I never got out of that bunk. I lived on crackers and water and that's it. We got into Panama and I came up on deck and the captain looked at me and says, 'Who are *you*?'

"Apprentice Seaman Duncan Brown, Sir."

George Moffett, radio technician 2/c: "When we went down to Panama, I took watch that night. Everybody wanted to go into Panama. All the time that I was on watch, why, they brought down fresh bananas. Also several five gallon cans of black paint. About midnight, here the crew comes back. Some of them get down the ladder all right and they start arguing with the crew that's going back up on the dock. Then they start throwing bananas back and forth at each other. That didn't work so good, so somebody took one of the five gallon cans of paint and dumped it down the side. One of the radiomen started down the ladder and, next thing you know, he's in whites with black paint all over them."

Louis Bobb, seaman 1/c: "That was the funniest thing, seeing this first class petty officer scraping paint off his liberty whites."

George Moffett: "He stripped down to his shorts and climbed the back of the shear so he could argue with the guys up on the dock because it was about at that level. And somebody says, 'Oh, you going swimming?'

"He turned around and he said, 'Yeah, I think I will.'"

"Then they got to betting as to whether he could stand on the shear and dive over without hitting the side. The beam of this thing is twenty-seven feet, which means to clear the shear on the center you've got to go

"I got seasick. I lay between the port two torpedoes in the forward torpedo room. I laid there for three days and all we did was roll from one side to the other. I never got out of that bunk. I lived on crackers and water and that's it." Duncan Brown

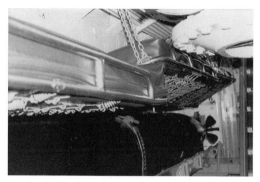

Bunks in the forward and after torpedo rooms were as tightly fit as everything else on Pampanito. *Note torpedo beneath bunk. Author*

out at least thirteen feet. He stood up there and he waved and he made it.

"Later, the shore patrol came down and I had them convinced that there wasn't anything really going on.

"No sooner did they leave than one of the guys threw a five gallon milk can down the hatch. We had guys sitting there playing cards.

"Then here comes another group, four guys in a shore patrol jeep. They start down this ladder with the paint on it and it turned them black. That started the fight all over again."

Duncan Brown: "We came back on board and we all brought back stalks, not hands, stalks of bananas. We were walking to the boat and we would very carefully walk hand over hand down this twenty-seven foot ladder to get to the deck of the boat. One of the guys on the dock is real smashed. The ladder is almost perpendicular. He walked from the dock to the deck, facing away from the ladder, with a stalk of bananas on his shoulder, and he never touched a thing except the rungs all the way down. He went straight to his bunk and fell asleep. The following morning when he came to, I told him, 'Say, you realize what you did last night?'

"He said, 'No.'

"I says, 'You come down that ladder, twenty-seven feet without falling off it.'

"'Can't happen.'

"When the tide went back out again, we came up on deck out of the galley. He looked and he saw the ladder there, and his eyes went up right up to the dock twenty-seven feet above and he just continued keeling right over and passed out."

Gordon Hopper, seaman 1/c: "When we left Panama, the last thing we waited for was the laundry truck to come down with the laundry. The truck came down and the laundry was all in wrapping paper, different guys' stuff, and they threw it all down in the torpedo room and we left.

When we got out to sea, we found we had all of ours, plus all another submarine's laundry."

The crossing to the Territory of Hawaii was easy, with calm seas and blue skies. It was late enough in the war that the enemy wasn't much of a threat in that part of the Pacific.

Upon arriving in Pearl Harbor, on Valentine's Day, 1944 *Pampanito* was laid up for a week for additional repairs and installations, including a five day haulout in drydock ARD #1 to renew and repair the wooden shaft hearings. While in Hawaii, on March 6, 1944, Charles Jackson was relieved of command, and Paul Summers was promoted to commanding officer.

Officers and crew were prepared as much as possible for the dangerous job that lay ahead. Day and night drills were conducted in the warm waters around Hawaii where practice torpedoes were fired, gun crews drilled, and many test dives were made. *Pampanito* even received a depth charging to give the crew a sense of what to expect.

Returning to Pearl Harbor, *Pampanito* was loaded with fuel and provisions. Sixteen Mark 14 steam torpedoes (called "steam fish" by the crew) were loaded into the forward torpedo room, and eight Mark 18 electric torpedoes were loaded into the after room. On March 15, 1944, exactly one year after her keel was laid down at Portsmouth, *Pampanito* left on her first war patrol.

3

BATTLEFIELD PACIFIC

The ending of every war sets the stage for the next one. Each side analyzes what worked and what didn't work — "lessons learned" they're called — devises new strategies, considers different tactics and develops new technologies. Each tries to anticipate who the next enemy will be, how he will act, and prepares plans for the conflict to come.

So it was with the United States Navy at the end of World War I. Naval planners examined the use of ships and submarines during that war. Large fleets of ships, from small destroyers to the mightiest dreadnoughts, met on the open sea. In some cases heavily-armed ships bombarded coastal defenses, forcing the tide of battle in their army's favor. Every sea battle, every shore bombardment was analyzed for errors in planning, communication and coordination. Ships were modified, defensive armor was strengthened. From this it was decided that the significant naval battles in future wars would take place between fleets of warships. The U.S. Navy, and every other major power, was

... command of the sea in the next war would be determined by "the great fleet battle" — a single, decisive naval attack.

convinced that command of the sea in the next war would be determined by "the great fleet battle" — a single, decisive naval attack. The most effective way to use warships was as a battle fleet; a central force of one or more battleships surrounded by supporting cruisers and destroyers. At the leading edge of this formation would be the submarine, used primarily for reconnaissance and intelligence gathering.

With their role thus defined, U.S. Navy submarine tactics before World War II focused on cautious attacks of enemy warships and battle fleets. There was some early concern about Germany's use of her submarines during World War I to cut Britain's supply lines, but that was believed to be an aberration. Most western nations considered it ungentlemanly for a submarine to "sneak up on" and sink a defenseless merchant ship. This feeling was so strong that international agreements signed in the 1930s restricted the use of undersea boats against merchant ships. At that time it was commonly understood that legitimate targets in future wars would only be warships.

Technology also played a part in preparations for future wars. Developed by the British during World War I, sonar was considered a very accurate means of detecting submarines.

SONAR

In 1917 the British set up the Allied Submarine Detection Investigation Committee to investigate the use of underwater sound transmission in locating submarines. The device was given a name made up of the first letters of the committee name — ASDIC. America's version was called sonar, for SOund NAvigation and Ranging. Basically, high-frequency sound waves are projected through hull-mounted sending/receiving microphones. If the sound wave struck an underwater object such as an enemy submarine, the sound echoed back to the sonar operator as a "ping." An experienced operator could determine the direction in which the submarine lay, its general distance away and speed and direction of travel.

A more passive device, which operated on the same principle, was the hydrophone which received underwater sounds such as propeller noises.

There were disadvantages. Sonar also revealed the presence and location of the ship sending the signal, and both devices lacked the ability to penetrate temperature gradients in the water, under which submarines could hide.

Before the outbreak of World War II, most western nations considered it ungentlemanly for a submarine to "sneak up on" and sink a defenseless merchant ship.

Any natural aggressiveness submarine commanders might have was tempered with caution because of belief in the accuracy and effectiveness of sonar in antisubmarine warfare. Frequent use of the periscope was discouraged and target data came almost exclusively from passive hydrophones, confirmed with brief glances through the periscope. If anything, submarines were considered an interesting adjunct to the battle fleet, but certainly not a major fighting machine.

With the attack at Pearl Harbor on December 7, 1941 naval warfare changed. New technology, in the form of the airplane, forced new strategies. Surprise attacks became standard. Fleets fought battles sometimes without ever seeing their enemy. The "gentlemanly" rules of war became a thing of the past. And the role of the submarine quickly became much more aggressive, much more important.

U.S. submarine commanders received the order from Washington: "Execute unrestricted air and submarine warfare against Japan." But, as with many things, it took some time for reality to catch up with intent. Submarine commanders, schooled in caution, had to retrain themselves and develop the aggressive mindset necessary for this new type of warfare.

As Japan advanced through the far Pacific, what remained of twenty-nine Allied submarines and three sub-tenders operating out of the Philippines fell back to more secure bases — first Java, then Fremantle, Australia. Under Captain John Wilkes, they became Submarines Southwest Pacific. The submarine fleet at Pearl Harbor consisted of sixteen fleet boats and six S-class submarines under Rear Admiral Charles A. Lockwood. The American submarine offensive then began from these two bases.

The first months of 1942 were spent overcoming the demoralizing and devastating effects of the loss of the Philippines, Wake Island and the Dutch East Indies. The fall of the Philippines and Wake Island, with so little resistance, led to the wholesale replacement of the cautious commanding officers in the submarine fleet. Men trained in passive pre-war tactics were relieved by younger, more aggressive officers. Officers more experienced with the torpedo data computer (TDC) replaced those who were not trained in its use or who were slow

TORPEDO DATA COMPUTER (TDC)

The Mark III Torpedo Data Computer gave American submarine commanders an edge over their German and Japanese counterparts. U.S. Navy

Before development of the Torpedo Data Computer, hitting an enemy ship with a torpedo was similar to trying to shoot at a moving target with a rifle. Once fired, the torpedo traveled in a straight line at a constant speed. If the target ship maintained a constant course and speed, it and the torpedo met at some point farther along the target's course line. But calculating where this point would be was extremely difficult, especially from a submerged boat limited to brief glimpses through the periscope to determine target information. The TDC changed all that.

The TDC was basically a mechanical computer made up of two sections: the position keeper and the angle solver. The position keeper tracked the target and calculated its position. It did so through automatic inputs of the submarine's course from the gyro compass and the submarine's speed from the pit log. Target length, estimated speed and angle on the bow could be input by cranks on the face of the machine. It also contained a sound bearing converter that calculated the target's location based on sonar. Additionally, when on the surface, the captain used his Target Bearing Transmitter (TBT), a rotating pair of binoculars attached to a gyro repeater on the bridge, to determine course, range and bearing which were automatically transferred to the

"There are two kinds of vessels at sea: submarines and targets."
Anon

TDC. Thus the position keeper kept constant track of the target's location at any given moment.

The angle solver took the target position from the position keeper and combined it with the characteristics of the torpedo and produced a constantly updated gyro angle for the torpedo. This was the angle from the submarine's heading that the torpedo would travel. The gyro angle was constantly updated automatically in each of the torpedo rooms. The TDC controlled both torpedo rooms and all ten torpedo tubes simultaneously.

The TBT gave target data from the bridge. San Francisco Maritime National Park Association

to comprehend it. In the last half of 1942, approximately forty submarine commanders out of 135 in the Pacific, about thirty percent of the entire force, were replaced. The earlier tactics of cautious submerged attacks on battle fleets quickly gave way to developing effective patrol methods of attack and aggressive destruction of commercial ships.

By mid-1942 sixty-seven submarines were available to American forces in the Pacific. But with the Japanese invasion of the Aleutians, military operations in the Solomons and reconnaissance missions in the

Japanese submarine I-173 did reconnaissance of Lahaina anchorage for the attack on Pearl Harbor. On January 27, 1942 she was located by Gudgeon *and sunk with a spread of three torpedoes, two of which found their mark. I-173 has the distinction of being the first warship ever sunk by an American submarine. Imperial War Museum.*

MARK 14 TORPEDO

Because the torpedo was such a devastating weapon during World War I, the world's navies increased the amount of armor plating on the sides of their larger warships. To overcome this, U.S. torpedo designers in the 1920s developed a magnetic detonator that went off when the torpedo was under the keel of a warship, a less-armored and more vulnerable area. In theory, the magnetism of the target's steel hull would set off the detonator. The U.S. Navy Bureau of Ordnance tested the device twice in 1926. It worked correctly once. The Navy nevertheless declared the test a success and certified the Mark 14 torpedo as its submarine weapon of the future. Unfortunately, in use, the torpedo failed miserably. During the last weeks of 1941 forty-five separate torpedo attacks failed because their weapons ran under the target without exploding, detonated too soon, or hit enemy ships without going off. Ninety-six torpedoes were fired and only three Japanese ships sunk. One Japanese merchant captain commented that his ship had so many dud torpedoes sticking out of the hull it looked like a porcupine.

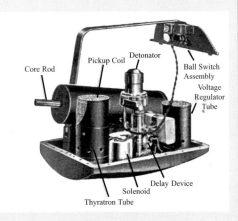

This Mark 8 Magnetic Exploder Mechanism is similar in construction to the Mark 6 which caused so many problems.. U.S. Navy

MARK 14 TORPEDO

The Mark 14 measured twenty-feet six inches in length and twenty-one inches in diameter. It carried a warhead consisting of 507 pounds of TNT (later 668 pounds of torpex) and weighed 2,215 pounds. Propelled by steam turbines it had two speed settings: 46 knots with a range of 4,500 yards, or 31.5 knots and a range of 9,000 yards. The Mark 8 exploder was designed to detonate either on impact or by magnetic induction when near the hull of a steel or iron vessel. Torpedoes were harmless until they had traveled about 450 yards when they automatically armed themselves.

SJ RADAR

Surface radar was one of the most important developments of World War II. Created by the Western Electric Company, submarine SJ radar could detect ships and planes at a distance of eight to twelve miles. More important, it wasn't affected by fog, haze, clouds or the dark of night. Its directional, high-gain antenna sent out a narrow, high frequency beam that swept the surface of the ocean to detect ships and low-flying planes. Targets were shown on two screens: a plan position indicator (PPI), a nine-inch cathode ray tube with a sweeping beam circling the screen like a clock and a five-inch "A" scope which was a CRT (Cathode Ray Tube) with a single horizontal trace. The PPI gave direction while the A scope gave distance. With SJ radar giving distance and direction of targets, submarine commanders could more easily avoid enemy planes and home in on Japanese shipping. High-speed night surface attacks increased from thirty to fifty-seven percent after radar was installed in the submarine fleet.

southwest Pacific there was little chance to put the new methods into practice. A few boats led the offensive into Japanese waters — *Gudgeon, Plunger* and *Pollack* being the first Pacific fleet submarines on offensive

JN25 — OPERATING CODE OF THE IMPERIAL JAPANESE NAVY

The first Japanese naval codes were broken by the U.S. Navy's cryptanalytic office in the mid-1920s. Japan countered in 1939 with a difficult machine-encoded cipher called "Purple." This was solved by the U.S. Army's chief cryptanalyst, William Friedman, who reverse-engineered the Japanese coding machine. By 1940 the Japanese messages were designated "Magic." This term was applied to all cryptographic intelligence until replaced by the British term "Ultra."

JN25 was a special naval code consisting of 33,333 naval terms, each represented by a different five-digit number, which, in turn, was coded with an additional five-digit number. In the first months of the Pacific war, the U.S. Navy had three stations that analyzed Japanese messages: station Negat in Washington, station Hypo at Pearl Harbor and station Belconnen in Melbourne. Joseph Rochefort at Hypo was able to solve JN25 enough to give Admiral Nimitz information critical to the Battles of Midway and the Coral Sea. As the war progressed, valuable information was given to American submarine commanders regarding the movement and location of Japanese ships.

war patrol. The results were disappointing. In two months three cargo ships and the Japanese submarine *I-173* were sunk. The total tonnage for 1942 was 735,000 tons, equal to two months' sinkings by U-boats in the Atlantic.

A major problem was the Mark-14 torpedo. Equipped with a magnetic detonator on the warhead, the torpedo was supposed to explode as it entered the target's magnetic field. Unfortunately, it didn't work as intended. Often the torpedoes were simply duds, bouncing off enemy hulls without exploding, or they blew up ineffectively when within a few hundred yards of the target, or they ran too deep, passing under the target without detonating at all. The problem was partly due to varying magnetic fields which differed according to latitude, and partly to faulty valves which caused the torpedoes to run as much as fifteen feet deeper than intended. It was not until 1943 that American submarines received a reliable torpedo.

By 1943 U.S. naval intelligence was growing adept at reading Japanese merchant and naval codes. American boats could be positioned to intercept Japanese warships and, just as important, Japanese merchant ship convoys. Geography was also an aid to submarine commanders. Most of the major shipping routes in the far Pacific funneled through narrow straits, making it much easier to locate enemy vessels. By the end of 1943 the U.S. submarine fleet had reliable torpedoes, surface search radar and almost twice as many boats as at the beginning of the war. Patrols routinely extended into the waters off Japan and along the East Indian trade routes. Three hundred Japanese merchant ships were sunk during a year that counted 700 patrols. Only fifteen U.S. submarines were lost. By the end of the year, Japan's merchant fleet would be reduced to less than 5 million tons, a million below the minimum necessary to supply her extended empire and war economy.

Japan's antisubmarine strategy was nonexistent during the first years of the war. Their merchant ships independently roamed the Pacific making any effort at protection difficult. Air patrols were set up over the East and South China Seas, but it wasn't until January 1944 that losses became so extensive that Japan began an escorted system of convoys. Termed the "Grand Convoy Fleet," she put some 150 escorts into service to protect her merchant ships. But the escorts lacked effective sonar and those few that were fitted with radar found it almost too primitive to be of

Part of Japan's ineffective "Grand Convoy Fleet," the Kaibokan-type escort No. 17 was sunk in January 1945. Measuring just over 206 feet long, she was propelled at 16.5 knots by twin diesels and carried 120 depth charges. Conway Maritime Press.

any use. The escorts became as vulnerable to submarine attack as the ships they tried to protect.

By 1944 the United States submarine fleet was able to broaden its attack strategy to include not only merchant ships (fifty-three ships totalling 280,000 tons in January alone), but warships when the occasion presented itself. American submarine commanders now had dependable torpedoes, effective radar, an excellent Torpedo Data Computer and accurate intelligence data from "Magic" intercepts. Three Japanese cruisers were sunk before August (*Tatsuta, Yubari, Oi*), two carriers went down during the Battle of the Philippine Sea (*Taiho, Shokaku*) and by the middle of November an additional five cruisers, a seaplane carrier and three light carriers fell to American torpedoes. The U.S. submarine fleet now included almost ninety boats operating out of Pearl Harbor and forty from Australia. Advance bases were set up in the Marshall and Admiralty Islands. Reducing the travel time necessary to reach the Japanese convoys, these bases put the rich oil tankers from Sumatra, Java and Borneo within reach of American submarines.

Sunk by torpedoes from USS Cavalla on June 19, 1944, the Shokaku had an unusually low profile because her exhaust stacks were directed horizontally over the starboard side. She displaced more than 32,000 tons and carried seventy-two aircraft. Conway Maritime Press

Fifty-six destroyers, escorts and patrol craft were lost to American submarines in 1944, with a loss of only eight submarines. It was into this theater and climate *Pampanito* eagerly entered, ready and anxious to do her part.

4

THE FIRST WAR PATROL
15 March - 2 May 1944

While training and equipment tests continued, *Pampanito* departed Pearl Harbor on her first war patrol. She was still at the "breaking in" stage where all the machinery, tools, equipment, electronics, parts, supplies and crew develop that essential fit and feel for one another to become one smoothly operating entity.

Earl Watkins, motor machinist's mate 2/c: "It was a time when you went from a boy to a man in a hurry, a time when you learn to be very responsible. Every man on board depended on you. Everyone had a very important job to do. Submarine sailors are a breed apart, a very special part of the Navy. We were family. Everyone on board was special. We were like brothers."

Joined by an escort vessel, *PC602*, Lt. Cdr. Summers pointed *Pampanito*'s bow toward Johnston Island, the first stop. A one square mile speck in the ocean located about 700 miles WSW of Honolulu, Johnston Island served as a staging area for U.S. submarines during

---

"Submarine sailors are a breed apart, a very special part of the Navy."

Earl Watkins

World War II. A brief test was made of the IFF (Identification Friend or Foe) device with a friendly plane. Lt. Cdr. Summers ordered a trim dive, to adjust the boat's trim, and, when it proved satisfactory, surfaced and continued on a west-southwesterly course.

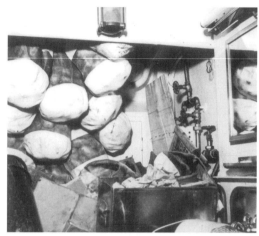

This view of sacks of potatoes stowed in the galley shows how tight space was on board, particularly at the beginning of patrol. San Francisco Maritime National Park Association.

During the next two days the crew spent their time drilling, testing equipment and preparing to enter the war. Arriving at Johnston Island on March 17, additional tests of the IFF were made with friendly planes and another trim dive was completed. Before the day ended, *Pampanito* dropped off her escort and sailed immediately for the far Pacific.

As she made her way westward from March 17 to March 21 (March 19 was lost when the boat crossed the International Dateline), *Pampanito* ran on the surface to take advantage of her greater speed and maneuverability. She could make just over twenty knots surfaced versus little more than eight when submerged. Each day was filled with training dives, practice fire control problems and emergency drills. Lt. Cdr. Summers was determined that his crew would be ready for any eventuality.

As they sailed farther west, the tension grew. Everyone knew they would soon be in dangerous waters where enemy submarines, planes and ships ruled the waves. At first,

---

IFF—IDENTIFICATION, FRIEND OR FOE

This was a radar-based system for identifying aircraft. Friendly planes were fitted with a transponder which, when it received a radar signal, automatically generated a series of pulses which showed up on the radar screen of the sender. These pulses identified the plane as friendly. If the plane was an enemy (foe) there would be no response or the radar image would not be the same as that of friendly planes.

danger came in fleeting glimpses. On March 22 a plane was spotted. Apparently *Pampanito* wasn't seen, for the aircraft quickly disappeared in the distance. Then, at 0640 the following morning another plane was picked up on the SD radar. It was nine miles out and closing. Summers ordered "Dive, dive, dive." With the claxon sounding, the crew disappeared down the conning tower hatch

> **SD RADAR**
> Less sophisticated than the SJ radar, the SD sent out a low-frequency omnidirectional non-rotating signal that was, nevertheless, adept at detecting airplanes. The target indicator was a five-inch cathode ray tube with a nonlinear sweep that was calibrated in miles.

and secured it even as the ocean poured over the places they stood moments before. At 0658 they surfaced. The plane was gone and they continued on their way. At 1030 the SD radar picked up another unidentified plane bearing due north at a range of eleven miles. Once again they dived, and, at 1050, resurfaced.

The following days were much the same as *Pampanito* neared her patrol area. She ran on the surface during the day. When planes were sighted, she dove and about half an hour later surfaced to continue her patrol. Now "breaking in" began in earnest. On March 25 a twin-engine Japanese "Lilly" bomber was sighted visually but did not show on the radar. A day later, another plane was seen but not picked up on the radar. Lt. Cdr. Summers noted in his War Patrol Log "Looks as though our SD radar might be improperly tuned." Then, while diving to 300 feet to avoid yet another plane the crew discovered the sea suction and discharge valves on the trim manifold were leaking badly. Outside pressure at this depth was 130 lb. per square inch.

As if that weren't enough, at the same time No. 6 torpedo tube flooded. After grinding in the bad suction and discharge valves, the boat surfaced at 1850 that evening to attend to the leaky torpedo tube. The torpedo was pulled and careful examination showed that although the exploder mechanism was dry, the after body was flooded. The crew removed the gyro steering and depth engines from the weapon, blew them dry with air, baked them to insure they were completely free of moisture, and reinstalled them. Meanwhile, Lt. Cdr. Summers ordered the boat stopped and put a diver over the side to examine the bad torpedo

"It was a time when you went from a boy to a man in a hurry, a time when you learn to be very responsible. Every man on board depended on you."

Earl Watkins

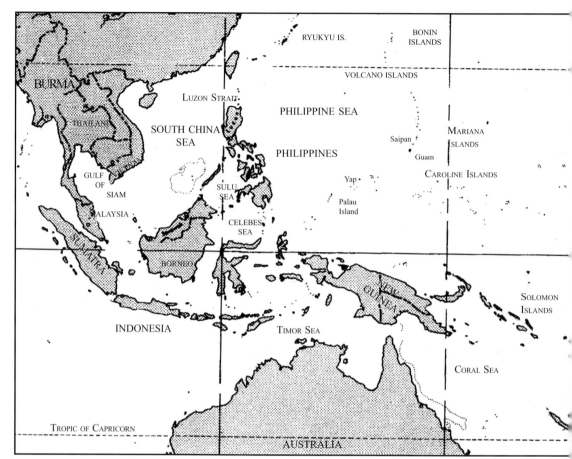

Pampanito's *patrol area on her first war patrol covered the Japanese trade supply route through Saipan Guam, Yap and Palau. Saipan is in the Mariana Islands and the route extends southwest toward the Celebe. Sea. U.S. Navy.*

tube. Everything on the outside was as it should be, meaning the leak was somewhere inside the tube.

Repairs to the tube were put off a day when, on March 27th, *Pampanito* entered her assigned patrol area. Now, for her own safety and for secrecy, she surfaced only at night. In fact the War Patrol log shows her diving at 0600 "for submerged daylight patrol covering Saipan-Palau and Saipan-Yap route." After cruising submerged all day she surfaced at 1903 and Lt. Cdr. Summers set a course of 235 degrees true to cover the Saipan-Palau route while heading in the general direction of Yap.

The leak in torpedo tube No. 6 continued and after cruising submerged all day on March 28, Lt. Cdr. Summers realized it would have to

be attended to that evening. Surfacing at 1831 he sent a crewmember inside the tube and discovered that a 3/8" pipe plug was missing from the forward roller housing of the tube. This left the roller housing and the tube itself directly open to the sea. The plug belonged in the superstructure just aft of the anchor chain locker, a vulnerable spot, because it meant a crewman would have to dive on the area from outside the boat. To do this they would have to stop and if caught stopped on the surface by the enemy, diving would take more time than they could safely allow. Worse yet, there was the possibility that if caught on the surface, there might not be time enough to retrieve the diver before submerging. But the repair was necessary.

At 2040 Capt. Summers ordered *Pampanito* stopped. Preparations were made to send the diver over. Then, at 2119 both the SD and SJ radars showed at least five large planes, six miles off, closing slowly. As a precaution Summers cleared the forecastle, post-poning the repair. When the range closed to four miles the moon came out and rather than get caught on the surface, Summers got underway and dived. After about thirty minutes he gave the order to surface. Sweeping the horizon with the periscope he was relieved to see everything clear. Within moments radar confirmed this. Once again the boat was stopped and over the side diving operations began.

Woodrow Weaver, torpedoman 1/c: "The leak was in a roller pocket in the forward part of the tube which extended outside the pressure hull.

"Our gunner's mate, Tony Hauptman, went over the side to secure the roller pocket as it was unbolted from inside the tube. The roller pocket was brought topside, taken to the pump room, repaired, and then replaced by Hauptman holding it in place while it was bolted in from inside the torpedo tube. It was a rather complicated but necessary operation. Without the repairs we would have been limited to five tubes forward instead of our normal six."

While this was going on 7 lb. of air pressure had to be kept in the torpedo room to keep the water out. At 2300 the repair was successfully completed and the boat continued its surface patrol toward Yap.

On March 30 the enemy got a little closer to *Pampanito*. At 0442 she dived after radar showed a contact (the second of the morning) moving in fast. A few minutes later a bomb explosion was heard, but not

---

Traditionally, the commanding officer of a vessel is referred to as captain, whether or not he holds that rank. Thus, Lt. Cdr. Summers is often referred to as Capt. Summers.

HOW DOES A SUBMARINE SUBMERGE?

Buoyancy is the upward force exerted by a liquid upon a floating body equal to the weight of water displaced by that body. Boats, ships, submarines, in fact, all watercraft, float because the force of buoyancy pushing upward is greater than the force of gravity pulling the vessel downward. Submarines submerge by overcoming this buoyant force. They do so by the use of ballast tanks. When on the surface the ballast tanks are full of air and the buoyant force is greater than that of gravity. To submerge, the air is let out of the tanks and replaced with water. The water increases the overall weight of the boat and the force of gravity increases to the point where it is greater than the buoyant force, allowing the submarine to submerge. This process is aided by use of the boat's hydroplanes or "planes" which are angled against the flow of water caused by the vessel's forward motion, bringing the bow down. Once submerged, the desired depth is attained by balancing the boat in a state of neutral buoyancy. This is called "catching a trim." The diving officer does this by adjusting the water level in the negative tank to a pre-determined level, taking into account fuel and stores consumption, density of the surrounding water (sea water varies in temperature and salinity both of which change its density) and a lot of experience. To surface, air is pumped into the ballast tanks once again allowing the buoyant force to overcome that of gravity.

---

close. While avoiding the plane, a serious leak was discovered in the hydraulic piping leading to the bow plane. Fortunately, it was in an easily accessible area, the CPO quarters. Although a considerable amount of oil was lost, the leak was repaired. It required silver soldering, which generated a lot of smoke — a serious condition inside an air-tight submarine. Fortunately, they were able to surface and take in fresh air. A few minutes later a twin-engine bomber was sighted and Capt. Summers again ordered, "Dive!" The boat remained submerged until nightfall.

Pampanito was assigned Lifeguard Duty on the last day of March. She patrolled a designated pattern south of Yap, watching for downed pilots returning from an American air raid. Three morning raids passed over on their way to bomb Palau, each returning about a half hour later. During the latter two return flights, signals were exchanged with the planes, in each case the pilots indicating no downed planes. The last

PERISCOPES

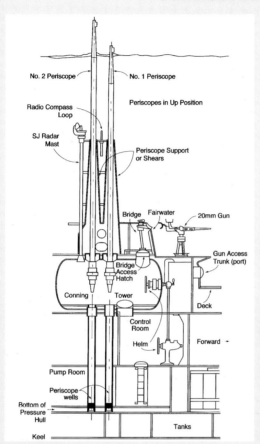

No. 2 Periscope

No. 1 Periscope

Periscopes in Up Position

Radio Compass
Loop

SJ Radar
Mast

Periscope Support
or Shears

Bridge   Fairwater   20mm Gun

Gun Access
Trunk (port)

Bridge
Access
Hatch

Conning   Tower

Deck

Control
Room

Helm   Forward

Pump Room

Periscope
wells

Bottom of
Pressure
Hull

Tanks

Keel

Here the periscopes are shown fully raised. When retracted they are flush with the top of the periscope shears. U.S. Navy

The purpose of a periscope is to give the conning officer a view of the waters around his vessel while submerged. A periscope consists of a vertical tube with a head prism inclined at a forty-five degree angle to the horizontal, a reducing telescope to encompass a wide field, and at the bottom of the tube an enlarging telescope and a lower prism facing the upper prism and parallel to it. The objectives of the two telescopes face each other. The periscopes on *Pampanito* were raised and lowered by cables powered by electric motors. Near the end of the war this was replaced with hydraulic power. The periscopes are about forty feet long. When lowered they rest on rubber bumpers at the bottom of the pressure hull. When raised, they pass through packing to prevent leaks. Several brass bearings provide support. They are filled with dry nitrogen to prevent fogging. The periscopes were also part of the fire control system and could be used to determine the range and bearing of the target. The attack or after scope is fitted with a range finder which gives the distance to the target. The forward scope is fitted with radar and provided very accurate target distances.

flight, at 1240, added an appreciative "thank you for standing by" to their message.

Released from Lifeguard Duty, *Pampanito* spent the first few days of April in the vicinity of Yap. During daylight hours the boat remained submerged while nighttime found her on the surface looking for enemy targets and ship movements. On April 1 all was quiet in Yap's harbor of Tomil when Capt. Sum-mers made a periscope reconnais-sance of the area. After circling the island, he again approached the harbor on the afternoon of April 3, this time coming within a mile and a half of the entrance buoys. Although there was a small DE (Destroyer Escort) moored to a wharf inside, there was no activity. That evening he surfaced and finding the area still quiet decided to cruise south of Yap to cover the Saipan-Palau route for any possible traffic.

The heart of the torpedo was the gyro which gave the weapon its direction when launched.   San Francisco Maritime National Park Association.

As before, there were fre-quent enemy plane sightings on the radar: a four-engined "Emily-type" bomber, a two-engined bomber and several others that caused the sub to dive each time to avoid detection. On April 4 a message was received from COMSUBPAC (COMmander SUBmarines PACific) ordering the boat to return to its assigned area. Apparently, it had wandered too far afield. April 5 and 6 were spent covering the Saipan-Palau route, ending in the southeast part of the assigned area. While submerged during the day, routine maintenance was done on the torpedoes. This was termed "routing the torpedoes" in the War Patrol log.

Anonymous crew-member No 1.[1]: "We had to do a routine. Torpedoes required a lot of maintenance. If the torpedo had been in the

---

[1] Some of the quotes come from a video tape made during a crew reunion in 1985. Those crewmembers not identified on the tape are indicated as "anonymous crewmember" in the text.

The Chidori *was a Tomozuru-class torpedo boat. These vessels were top-heavy and notoriously unstable. They carried three 5in/50s and could do thirty knots. Conway Maritime Press.*

tube too long, we'd have to pull them out and routine it, check various things, that it was operating right. Check the air pressure in the air flask: 3,000 lb. a square inch. And we had to watch for moisture if you went from a cool area to the tropics and vice versa. So they required a lot. Electric torpedoes, we had to watch because hydrogen would come off the batteries. We had to keep them charged and all that."

Just after noon on April 7, *Pampanito's* radar operator picked up a target about ten miles off the starboard bow. Through the periscope Lt. Cdr. Summers first sighted a "coal-burning freighter similar to *Hokuyo Maru.*" He estimated the ship at about 4,200 tons and she was being escorted by a *Chidori*-type torpedo boat. Lowering the periscope, he came to the normal approach course, set the motors at standard speed and waited twenty minutes, then raised it again. Now he saw a second small freighter in column astern of the first, with the escort on the port bow of the leading ship. The small convoy was zig-zagging on a base course of about 240 degrees and making a speed of 12 knots. Summers moved the submarine into attack position.

1326 - Set up looks fairly good, came left to 110 degrees for about 75 degrees starboard track on leading target. The escort is crossing over toward us from port to starboard bow of the target. A second look disclosed a small mast well astern and to starboard of second ship in the column, probably another escort.
1330 - With a track of about 75 degrees starboard, zero gyro angle and torpedo run of about 1400 yards, up periscope for a final check on set-up, disclosing the following: leading escort was heading almost directly for us at a range of less than 500 yards, leading target was zigging away to the left, with smoke billowing from his stack.

Summers took *Pampanito* down and a minute later a single first depth charge was heard, although it wasn't close. He was puzzled that

the escort picked him up because he was very cautious in his periscope observations, limiting their duration to the minimum amount of time needed to get data for the firing solution. Afterward, he decided they must have heard the air noises involved in getting the torpedo tubes ready. The Japanese escort probably had a very skilled sonar operator. At 1345 Summers started up to periscope depth, but his sound man reported the escort approaching from astern with a second target coming on the port quarter. Three minutes later *Pampanito* received two depth charges close to starboard and above her. Summers took her deep.

> 1403 - 1405 - Received a string of five depth charges varying in depth from 150 to 600 feet, all <u>very</u> close with two straddles. During this interval we heard the screws of one escort through our hull, and the sound man distinctly made out a definite ping similar to a fathometer as the escort passed over us and let go his charges. This string of five depth charges caused considerable damage and shaking up of the boat.
>
> 1406 - We can definitely hear the two escorts now pinging on us.

The force of the explosions was enough to knock those who weren't holding on, to the deck plates. The boat rocked with their force, heavy steel bulkheads springing in then out again. Deck plates and gratings jumped from their beds while pipelines vibrated with odd humming noises. The concussion was stunning, causing some of the crew to see stars. Others were awed at the fog of cork bits, dust and paint shaken loose from the bulkheads. In a similar experience on another boat, Capt. Edward L. Beach, author of *Submarine!*, said, "The whole hull rings and shudders, whips and shakes itself, bounces sideways, up and down."

At a *Pampanito* crew reunion in 1985 Capt. Summers remembered it this way: "We had a convoy coming out of Guam and I was a little full of tea and ginger, whatever you want to call it, and we made a good approach. It was a very calm sea and late afternoon and I even went deep to find a gradient where after I was sure we'd be depth-charged after we attacked. I came up, I knew where my gradient was, there wasn't much, we started in and then I said I'll take a periscope look and then we're going to shoot. Well I stuck up the periscope, we were 1400 yards away, and the only thing I could see was the bow wake of the damn escort.

"The whole hull rings and shudders, whips and shakes itself, bounces sideways, up and down."

Capt. Edward L. Beach

Well, he let us have it, and dropped one just to let us know he had us located. We went under the convoy and I came up and I said, all right we'll get on the other side. Well, before we even got out there they let us have it. They dropped three depth charges close to us, flooded out the whole shear, knocked out my periscopes, knocked out my sonar gear, flooded the main induction, flooded all but one torpedo. We were lucky it was getting late in the afternoon, so we finally pulled clear and it took us three days just to get back to where we could dive."

Norman Arcement, engineman 3/c: "The first time we got depth charged was the worst. That was the time I thought I was dead. I couldn't see. The light bulbs broke and it was all dark. I took a flashlight and shined it towards my face and something was over my face and I didn't feel it because I had the head phones over my head and I couldn't see the lights in the flashlight. I couldn't see the lights in the boat and I said, 'Holy smoke, I must be dead! I can't see anything."

Charles A. McGuire, Jr., Yeoman 1/c: "When you were being depth charged, you were all frightened out of your wits. We used to crack jokes to relieve tensions. You couldn't do anything about it."

Most of the crew found the experience terrifying, although they tried not to show it. Some said a silent prayer. Some described it as "mind-boggling."

Gordon Hopper, seaman 1/c remembered it as his most frightening experience of all the boat's patrols. "We became attackee before we could fire a fish. Two excellent Japanese sub chasers depth charged us more violently than any other attack on us. For many of us this was our introduction to submarine combat. Not a happy introduction."

Woodrow Weaver: "It was my depth charge baptism of fire. The exploding depth charges caused the sub to vibrate for its entire length. I don't recall being especially frightened; we were too busy checking valves and assessing damage to be scared."

For the next two hours Summers stayed at deep submergence trying to escape the enemy escorts. They were persistent, "coming in and going out intermittently." He tried to locate a temperature gradient (which would deflect the enemy sonar signals) to hide under but none was found. Finally, at 1600, the sound man reported high speed screws moving away. *Pampanito* slowly rose to periscope depth. Her trim was heavy, she had more weight forward than aft, but Summers resisted the

urge to start the trim pumps, lest the noise alert the escorts, should they still be lurking above. At 1640 he cautiously raised the periscope. A quick sweep revealed a clear horizon. It was safe to surface and he did so twenty minutes later. By then the convoy was a good forty miles ahead, so, estimating their course at 230 to 240 degrees, he pursued at full speed while maintaining a high periscope watch.

Woodrow Weaver: "We had suffered some damage, some of which was readily apparent, also other damage which did not show up until later."

By early the next morning it was evident the convoy was lost. After sending a contact report to COMSUBPAC, Summers headed north to resume patrol on the Saipan-Palau route and dove before daylight.

During the day, Summers held a brief crew meeting. Anonymous crewmember No. 2: "He called us together after that shellacking we took and he says, 'Fellas, I never took a shellacking like this in my life. I don't intend to take another like it. But if you don't think I won't sacrifice this crew and boat if the prize is worth it, just think again. I will.'

"Up to that time we'd dive and of course we'd just go to periscope depth or a little below, maybe a hundred feet. After that, after we took that shellacking on the first run, Pete [Capt. Summers] said, 'Take her down. Take her deep. First stop 600 [feet].'"

While patrolling submerged, the torpedoes were inspected and again "routined." During the day it was discovered that the torpedo in No. 2 tube had a flooded exploder and those in tubes No. 5 and No. 6 had flooded after bodies. All the others were dry. The shock from the depth charging the previous day also caused the boat's exhaust valve leak seals to break. Later in the day it was discovered that one of the Mark 18 torpedoes in the after torpedo room had two cracks in a section of the battery cells, a result of the same depth charging.

Routining of the torpedoes was completed the following day and those in tubes 5 and 6 had their gyros, steering engines and depth engines cleaned, baked and oiled.

Toward the end of the midnight-to-four watch on April 10, a convoy was picked up on radar at twelve miles out. The radar tracking party was posted and it soon developed that there were two large ships with four escorts: one ahead, one astern and one on each flank. The two

"When you were being depth charged, you were all frightened out of your wits. We used to crack jokes to relieve tensions."
Charles A. McGuire

large ships were zig-zagging on a base course of 195 degrees at a speed of nine knots. Summers began an end around, maneuvering to position himself in front of the convoy.

Shortly after 0900 *Pampanito* was in position, just under eighteen miles ahead of the convoy. Submerging, Summers went down to 400 feet looking for a temperature gradient or inversion layer under which to escape after his attack. There was none. Just before 0930 the boat was at fifty feet maintaining a periscope and sound watch. At 1020 the sound of echo ranging was picked up. At 1030 smoke was seen over the horizon in the direction of the convoy. Summers began his approach. As the convoy came into view, he made out two large freighters, about 7,000 tons each, similar to the *Tuyama Maru* and *Tokiwa Maru* found in the ONI manual 208-J.[2]

There were three destroyers, one ahead and one on each flank with a subchaser following astern. Summers identified the destroyers as the Fubuki-type. He decided to pass under the destroyer screen at a depth of 100 feet, then turn right for a stern shot at the leading target. But once in position for the shot he found that the leading destroyer had dropped back on the port bow of his target, making two destroyer screens on the same side as *Pampanito*. Because they ranged back and forth ahead and astern of the boat, Summers decided to come left, instead, for a bow shot on the second freighter. But by the time he was in position, the convoy had zigged away and was out three miles. Not one to give up, he waited until they were below the horizon, then surfaced and did another end around, hoping to make an attack after dark.

Surfacing at 1339, Summers brought the boat up to full speed and began the end around maneuver. By 1925 he was in position ahead of the convoy. Within a few minutes he had the convoy coming on the radar scope at eleven miles out zigzagging on a base course of 125 degrees and in the same disposition as earlier. As the moon was just coming up, he decided to come in on the convoy's starboard bow away from the moon. Just before 2100 he began his approach. At 2154 he was in position with the target about 2,500 yards out and the nearest destroyer at 1,000 yards.

---

[2] Published by the Office of Naval Intelligence, this manual gave silhouettes and characteristics of almost every ship in the Japanese merchant fleet.

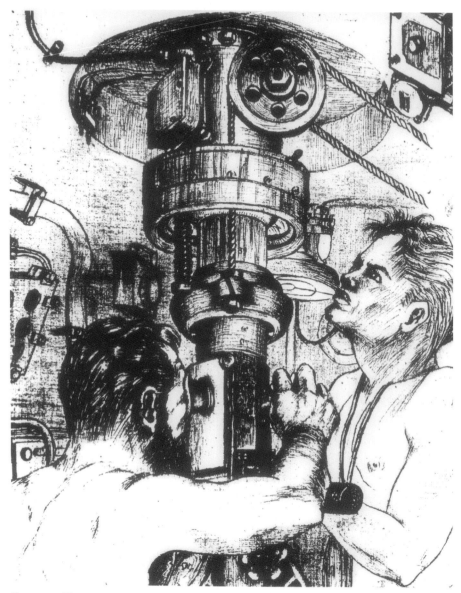

Crewman Tony Hauptman was Pampanito*'s artist. Here, he accurately captured the intensity of acquiring a target through the periscope. San Francisco Maritime National Park Association.*

2155 - Fired a spread of 4 torpedoes designed to get 2 hits. Track 81 degrees starboard, torpedo run 2450 yards, gyro angle 18 to 20 deg. left. With a quick set-up on leading destroyer, fired two torpedoes, track 102 starboard, torpedo

Fubuki-class destroyers were rated at 38 knots. In addition to depth charges they carried six 5in/50s. Conway Maritime Press.

run 2,400 yards, gyro angle 17 deg. right. Noted starboard DD [destroyer] screen coming in fast on our port beam, too close for comfort. Evidently the DD at which I had just fired had "gotten the word too" for he is coming right rapidly.

2156 angle on bow of leading DD is about 20 deg. starboard now.

2156-10 - Commenced evasive tactics.

2156-40 - First torpedo hit with violent explosion felt throughout the ship. Target was probably carrying high test gas in his tanks.

2l56-58 - Second torpedo hit. These two explosions time exactly with the first and second torpedo runs to target and were the two torpedoes of the spread to hit the target if the setup was correct.

2157 Sound reported target screws had stopped. Also destroyer on our port beam coming in fast.

2159 - First depth charge; not close.

2200 - Much noise, confusion and milling around in the direction of the target.

2201 - Pattern of three depth charges, fairly close. At about 300 feet, commenced taking in water through main air induction piping. #9 torpedo tube indicating sea pressure. Evidently the outer door is leaking from the last depth charging.

2202 - Pattern of three depth charges, fairly close.

2203 - Another depth charge. Only two of the four screen seem to be searching for us. There is still much noise coming from direction of the target. One escort seems to be circling target.

2205 - Had to close the hull induction drains in the engine rooms and the maneuvering room as water is coming in too fast. Boat is getting very heavy. One of the poppet valves in the forward torpedo room stuck open on firing causing flooding of the torpedo room bilges.

2207 - 0030 Intermittent depth charges. None very close. A total of about 25 were dropped. Am having to use between 90 and 100 shaft turns with a 12-15 degree rise bubble to keep the boat from going any deeper. Have not been able to find an injection temperature gradient.

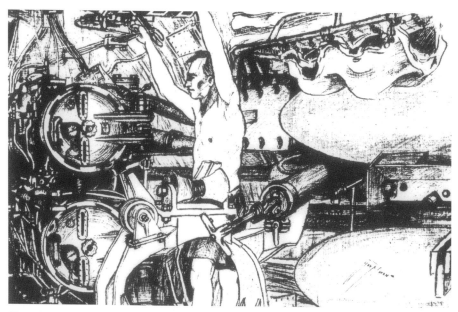

Tony Hauptman's rendering of the torpedo room shows how tight the interior of the boat was and how the crew dressed during patrol. San Francisco Maritime National Park Association.

2315 - Both sound head training motors grounded out due to bilge water running over the forward torpedo room deck with a 15 degree rise bubble. Tried using a bubble in the safety tank twice to hold my depth, and each time it brought the DD's over again. Excessive noise being caused by the pressure forcing water into main induction piping around the leaking flange rubber gaskets.

11 April 1944
0015 - Destroyer screws going away.
0043 - Surfaced. All clear.

According to Woodrow Weaver, as they dove to avoid this depth charging, the damage caused by the attack on them a week earlier began to show. "The earlier attack had weakened gaskets in our main induction lines which ran outside the pressure hull and supplied air to the engine rooms when we operated on the surface. At deep submergence the induction lines started taking on water. With the induction lines flooded, we were too heavy to maintain depth control and slowly went deeper and

2205 - Had to close hull induction drains in the engine rooms and maneuvering room as water is coming in too fast. Boat is getting very heavy.

deeper. The test depth of the *Pampanito* was 400 feet. The additional weight of water from the flooded lines forced us down to 600 feet."

The air conditioning was shut down for silent running. The temperature soon rose above 120°F, Men glowed eerily with sweat in the emergency lighting while bulkheads and decks glistened with condensation and seawater seeped in through valve seats and propeller shaft stuffings. The boat, creaking and groaning, was well below her test depth.

Woodrow Weaver: "At that point the C.O. [commanding officer] ordered the safety tank partly blown. (The safety tank is a tank located about amidships and of heavier construction to allow for more pressure when being blown.) The shot of air into the safety tank expelled enough weight of water to check our descent. The sub then started to rise and the rate of ascent could not be controlled. As we came up, the air under pressure in the safety tank was expanding and forcing out more water. The only way to correct the problem was to vent enough air out of the tank to control the amount of water. We could not vent the tank outboard to sea because we had a Jap destroyer looking down our throats. The skipper then tried venting the tank inboard — inside the submarine. Venting inboard was raising the pressure inside the boat. The vent was too small and we could not vent the tank fast enough. The result was we could not maintain depth control, and were forced to the surface with a Japanese destroyer just a few miles away on the horizon.

"A submarine does not have much freeboard and it difficult to see when only the conning tower is out of the water. Luckily for us, it was beginning to get dark. The skipper ordered one diesel engine started with the air supply coming through the open conning tower hatch. The normal air supply was cut off by the flooded induction lines. With propulsion provided by one engine, we slowly made our exit from the area."

The boat wasn't handling the way it should, so rather than pursue the enemy, Summers pulled away to evaluate the damage. Even a preliminary inspection showed *Pampanito* took a beating. The outboard air induction was completely flooded, both sound head training motors were grounded out and a Mark 18 torpedo in tube No. 9 was flooded.

A contact report was sent to USS *Harder*, known to be nearby, in the hopes that she could verify *Pampanito*'s target was missing and had

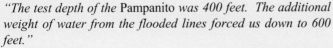
"The test depth of the Pampanito *was 400 feet. The additional weight of water from the flooded lines forced us down to 600 feet."*

                                        Woodrow Weaver

therefore sunk, and so that she could sink the other freighter. COMSUB-PAC was also notified.

By sunrise Summers had submerged the boat and was patrolling in a northerly direction covering the Guam-Palau route while making a more thorough evaluation of damage. Several leaking flange fittings were found in the outboard air induction piping; many of the flanges had loose bolts on them. In addition, they couldn't get the torpedo out of No. 9 tube.

Surfacing after sunset, work parties began repairs. The loose bolts on the flanges were tightened. Using a jury rig, the torpedo was pulled from No. 9 tube. Once out in the open they saw that the weapon was completely flooded and the warhead casing was dished in in several places. The battery cells were cracked, deformed and completely flooded. These were thrown overboard while the other parts of the torpedo were dried and kept on board. The real problem was the sound head training motors. They were unsalvagable. Without them the boat's sonar would point only in one direction, rather than rotate in all directions. However, one of the electricians' mates remembered that the boat's lathe had the same type of motor and suggested using it.

On April 12 *Pampanito* dived at sunrise for her normal patrol of the Saipan-Palau route. Summers took her down to 250 feet and found the same leaks as before. This meant he would have to avoid deep submergence for the rest of the patrol. This was cause for anxiety because going deep was their best means of escaping depth charging.

The following day the lathe motor was installed as a sound head training motor and, fortunately, seemed to be working.

Anonymous crewmember #1: "We had a fella by the name of Langin, an electrician. He was real good. We got this heavy motor and we says, 'We're going to get two men with a pipe and we're going to hoist this thing up and move it.'

"And Langin said, 'Get the hell out of the way.'

"Langin picked up the motor and carried it all the way forward."

Anonymous crewmember #2: "He carried it the length of the sub. Where did it come from? It came off of the lathe."

Although his boat was damaged, Summers continued his search for enemy targets. He noted in the War Patrol Log that the Saipan-Palau route was completely unproductive and patrolled the southeastern part of

"We could not vent the tank outboard to sea; because we had a Jap destroyer looking down our throats. The result was we could not maintain depth control, and were forced to the surface with a Japanese destroyer just a few miles away on the horizon."
Woodrow Weaver

his assigned area, covering the southwestern approach to Guam and Saipan. Finding no targets he once again cruised toward the Saipan-Palau route and spent the next several days searching back and forth between the two areas. Other than diving at the approach of the usual enemy airplane traffic, there was little activity.

On April 18 the SJ radar went out and was repaired two days later. Low on fuel, Summers contacted COMSUBPAC on April 20 to advise them that he didn't have enough to return to Pearl Harbor. Two days later they directed him to head for Midway to refuel. The crew's relief at leaving the war zone was short-lived when at noon they dove to avoid an enemy plane and heard three bomb explosions well astern. They weren't out of danger yet.

That evening, their voyage home was interrupted again when they were once more assigned to Lifeguard Duty covering the southern routes approaching Guam and Saipan. *Pampanito* patrolled this area until April 25. During this time a saltwater leak was discovered in the No. 1 main engine exhaust, causing the engine to be shut down for the remainder of the patrol. That evening two small enemy patrol boats were seen heading toward Guam but were avoided due to the ongoing lifeguard operation.

April 25 was a day of confusion. At noon a formation of American Liberators [B-24 bomber] was seen heading on a southeasterly course. There was no word of any planes down, although there was no official notification of this. Later in the afternoon enemy planes were spotted on radar and after diving, *Pampanito*'s crew heard two bomb explosions, one fairly close. Fortunately the lifeguard mission was completed and they could remain submerged the remainder of the day. At 2245 that evening Summers sent his departure report to COMSUBPAC.

En route to Midway on April 26 and 27, the boat continued avoiding enemy planes and bombs, diving three times the first day and once on the second to avoid a reported periscope nearby.

April 28 revealed a miscalculation in the fuel supply. Apparently there were 6,000 less gallons on board than originally thought. To conserve fuel, the remainder of the leg home was at "one engine speed."

Relief finally came on April 29 when no planes or enemy vessels were spotted, and *Pampanito* was able to cruise the rest of the way to Midway on the surface. Arriving there at 1430 on the afternoon of May 2, she took on 20,000 gallons of diesel fuel. Seven Mark 18 and ten Mark 14

Duncan Brown, electrician, left and Joe Eichner, cook, opening the galley hatch at Midway, May 4, 1944. San Francisco Maritime National Park Association.

Mod 3A torpedoes were sent ashore. The following day an additional 10,000 gallons of fuel were taken aboard along with two Mark 14 Mod 3A torpedoes.

Departing Midway at 1300 on May 4, *Pampanito* arrived at Pearl Harbor on May 8, 1944, after fifty-four days at sea.

Woodrow Weaver: "One of the morale boosting features employed by COMSUBPAC was to have each sub returning from patrol met by the submarine base band. It was a good feeling to have a brass band serenading the crew as they tied up to the dock.

"Another was the handling of the mail. While on patrol, the sub base post office separated each man's mail and tied it into a bundle. On arrival at the pier, the first thing which came on board was the mail. The bundles of mail were passed out, and all activities halted until the crew had time to read letters from home."

Crates of fruit, celery, lettuce and other fresh produce were laid out on the dock. Ice cream and cool drinks were provided. Ned Beach, who served on *Wahoo* and *Trigger*, described it: "It was not at all uncommon to see a bearded sailor, pockets stuffed with apples and oranges, reading letter after letter in quick succession and munching on a celery stalk …"

Woodrow Weaver: "Most patrols averaged about sixty days and submarines were provisioned for about that period of time. The greatest problem was in finding space for the food. Submarine food was the best in the Navy, and submarine cooks took great pride in their job of upholding that reputation. They tried their best to anticipate what and how much submarine sailors would consume in sixty days and ordered

"On arrival at the the pier, the first thing which came on board was the mail. The bundles of mail were passed out, and all activities halted until the crew had time to read letters from home."

Woodrow Weaver

Fresh water was precious on board. Many of the crew didn't shave. Here most of the crew pose at Midway, May 4, 1944 for a group photo while berthed alongside USS Proteus. *Front row, left to right: Frank Lederer, Joseph Austin, Robert Matheny, Roger Bourgeois, Lloyd MacVane, James Behney; second row, left to right: Renard Lombardi, Louis Bobb, Hubert Brown, Edmund Stockslader, William McCollum, Frank Michno, Duncan Brown, Otto Aimone, John Wilson, Clarence Carmody, Harold Chinn, William Yagemann, Norbert Kaup; third row, left to right: Irving Costello, Roger Walters; fourth row, left to right: Bernard Zalusky, Lynn Martin, Edward Tonkin, Walter Cordon, Robert Bennett, William Canty, Albert Van Atta, Lawrence Langin, Milton Meyers, Anthony Hauptman, Paul Pappas; fifth row, left to right: Theodas King, Ralph Attaway, Gordon Hopper, Ralph Herber, Isaac Robinson; back row: Ray Mosey. San Francisco Maritime National Park Association.*

their supplies accordingly. They could not always deal with the whims of sailors, however.

"It was always a submarine custom for sailors to have access to food at all times, and on this particular patrol someone, on the first night out, mixed up a batch of tuna fish and mayonnaise. The idea caught on and every night someone was mixing up the same thing. The result was we soon ran out of canned tuna. The poor cooks had to put up with a lot of griping the remainder of the trip.

"Even our laundry service was not neglected. Fresh water is at a premium on a submarine. There is little for bathing, and virtually none for laundry. Before going on patrol, each sailor stocked enough dungarees and underwear to last for the sixty days without having to launder them. On arrival in port, each crew member had a big bag of dirty clothes. These were promptly carted off to the sub base laundry where they did an outstanding job. Our laundry was always back within two days with all rips and tears in clothing neatly mended. Someone said you could send two buttons to the base laundry and they would be returned with a shirt attached.

"At the start of the war, the Navy took over the Royal Hawaiian Hotel, on Waikiki Beach, in Honolulu. The hotel was used for rest and recreation for submarine crews after their patrols. The routine at the end of a patrol was to read your mail, send soiled clothing to the laundry, turn the sub over to a relief crew which would make necessary repairs and head to the Royal Hawaiian Hotel for two weeks. At the hotel, food was served all day long. We were quartered two men to a room, and had nothing to do for two weeks. We could swim on the beach at Waikiki, play tennis or just loll in the sun. After two weeks at the hotel, we were refreshed and ready to go again. It is said the submarine force is a young man's navy. I think it was especially true during the war. The older fellows — those past thirty-five years of age — did not snap back as readily as the twenty year old sailors."

"You could send two buttons to the base laundry and they would be returned with a shirt attached." Woodrow Weaver

5

THE SECOND
WAR PATROL
3 June - 23 July 1944

While the crew unwound on the beach at Waikiki, *Pampanito* went through a major repair and refit. Damages incurred during the voyage were repaired and modifications were added. Main Ballast Tank No. 4 was converted to a variable tank. As such it would carry fuel oil at the beginning of a patrol, be flushed out when the fuel was gone and again become a ballast tank. This conversion extended her patrol range by 2,500 miles. A dead reckoning tracer (DRT) was installed in the conning tower. This automatic plotting device was the second such unit on board. Finally, a VHF (Very High Frequency) radio system was installed. This line-of-sight radio was ideal for short range communications with airplanes while on Lifeguard Duty, and with other submarines while operating in wolf packs. The extremely short range limited the possibility of Japanese ships or planes homing in on transmissions.

USS Proteus *(AS-19) as she appeared on August 8, 1960 after conversion to an FBM tender. U.S. Navy.*

After two luxurious weeks of R&R at the Royal Hawaiian Hotel, about one third of the crew from the first patrol were transferred; assigned to new construction in the States, became part of the relief crews at the sub base or were billeted on sub tenders. The remaining crew returned to *Pampanito* at the submarine base at Pearl Harbor. The relief crew filled them in on the repairs made and what needed to be done to prepare for the next patrol. To acclimate the new crew to the old and to acquaint the entire crew with new equipment and repairs, two weeks of training exercises were held in Hawaiian waters.

On June 1, 1944 Summers received new orders. *Pampanito*'s next patrol would be off the home waters of Japan, searching the shores of Kyushu, Shikoku and Honshu for targets. *Pampanito* sailed for Midway Island two days later, escorted by *PC485*. There, she rendezvoused again with the sub tender *Proteus* (AS-19), a repair and supply ship, to undergo periscope, radar and valve repairs and take on 20,000 gallons of fuel oil. Departing Midway on June 8, *Pampanito* headed for her patrol area at two engine speed. The slower speed (four engine speed was maximum) was to conserve fuel because of the increased distance she would travel getting to and from the Japanese coast.

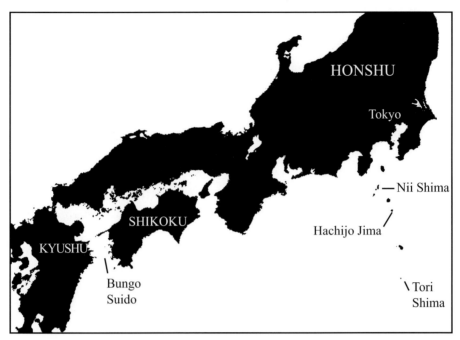

Pampanito entered her patrol area near Tori Shima, steering just south of west toward the southern coast of Kyushu. Arriving there June 19 she patroled east northeast along the coast departing just north of Tori Shima on July 18.

Remembering that tuna with mayonnaise was the popular item on the first patrol, and not wanting to suffer the wrath of the crew, the cooks laid in a large supply for the second war patrol. But there was no way to anticipate the whims of submariners. Woodrow Weaver, torpedoman 1/c: "They put canned tuna in every nook and cranny. The sailors wouldn't touch it. On that patrol, chocolate mixed up with canned condensed milk caught everyone's fancy. We soon ran out of condensed milk, which was a disaster, as most sailors used it in their coffee. The poor cooks were in hot water again. Theirs was a losing battle."

June 9 was omitted from the calendar as *Pampanito* crossed the International Date Line on her way to patrol off the southern coast of Japan. Although experiencing high seas and typhoon-like winds, she reached her patrol area on June 15, sighting the Japanese island of Tori Shima.

Cliff Grommet, First Lieutenant: "I had the deck on the surface at two a.m. when approaching the coast of Japan. We were going past one of the armed islands off the coast and I was sure glad when we got by without trouble."

"Chocolate mixed up with canned condensed milk caught everyone's fancy. We soon ran out of condensed milk, which was a disaster, as most sailors used it in their coffee."
Woodrow Weaver

The foul weather continued. Navigation was difficult because star sights were unavailable due to the weather. Nevertheless, she moved westward, then, reaching the islands off the southern tip of Japan, turned east northeast to begin her search of coastal routes for targets.

As *Pampanito* penetrated farther into enemy waters, she maintained the routine established in her first patrol — staying submerged during the day and surfacing at night. In this way she was able to recharge her batteries and freshen the breathing air at night while avoiding enemy ships and planes during the day. It was summer, however, and daylight lasted much longer than darkness. This meant the boat was submerged for sixteen hours a day and spent only eight hours each night on the surface.

Woodrow Weaver: "This patrol took the most out of the crew from a physical standpoint. We had to submerge around four o'clock in the morning and could not surface until eight o'clock in the evening. The only air available to us was what was trapped in the submarine compartments when we dived. After twelve hours or so, the air would become bad because of the depletion of oxygen. Carbon dioxide would build up to the point deep breathing was required to get enough oxygen to satisfy body requirements. We had a carbon dioxide absorbent, in powder form, which was spread to take up some of the CO_2. It helped to some degree, but the last hours of each day were very weakening and uncomfortable. We looked forward to night fall and surface operations when we could get some fresh air.

"On surfacing each evening, we went through a routine of taking an air suction through the boat to clear out all the stale air on board. The routine of clearing out the stale CO_2 after a day's submerged operations required opening the forward torpedo room hatch, which provided access to the main deck and was normally closed at all times while at sea. The conning tower hatch was closed as well as the main induction valve which supplied air to the induction lines for the motors. The result was only one source of air to the engines and that was through the open torpedo room hatch. The air flow was through the length of the submarine to the engines. The engine air suction created a small gale through the compartments clearing out the stale air in a hurry. Papers, blankets and anything loose sometimes wound up in the engine rooms.

"We had to submerge around four o'clock in the morning and could not surface until eight o'clock in the evening. The only air available to us was what was trapped in the submarine compartments when we dived."

Woodrow Weaver

View of engine room showing one engine and instrument panel. Pampanito *has two engine rooms, each containing two main engines. Author.*

"My job during these air purifying operations was to open the forward hatch and sit there to make sure it remained open as long as a suction was being taken through the boat. The hatch could not be closed until the main induction valve was opened and the engines had access to their normal source of air. If the hatch had been closed during the operation, severe physical damage could have been suffered by the crew. The best part of the job was sitting there in the fresh air and looking at lights on the beach. It seemed a bit bizarre to me that I was looking at lights in Japan during the war."

On those few occasions when *Pampanito* did travel on the surface during daylight hours, lookouts kept a watchful eye so that she could dive if an enemy plane was spotted or a target moved into range. A constant menace in this area were the small patrol boats that seemed to constantly cruise just offshore.

On June 23, *Pampanito* approached Bungo Suido, the straits between the large Japanese islands of Kyushu and Shikoku. This had been a very productive area for American subs on earlier patrols and was known as the "Hit Parade" among submariners. In the distance the coastline of the Japanese homeland was visible.

"The best part of the job was sitting there in the fresh air and looking at lights on the beach. It seemed a bit bizarre to me that I was looking at lights in Japan during the war."

Woodrow Weaver

The Japanese shore and coastal islands were well-fortified but they weren't the only danger to *Pampanito*. At night, in the mirrorlike sea, luminescent marine life glowed green at the slightest disturbance. The boat's motion through the water left a long, arrow-shaped green glow behind that pointed directly at her. The smallest ripple, even flying fish skittering out of the sub's way, sent sparks across the water.

But at times this phenomenon also worked in *Pampanito*'s favor. One night, at 0350, the officer of the deck, the navigator, and one of the lookouts sighted the phosphorescent wake of a torpedo crossing *Pampanito*'s bow. Left full rudder was ordered at flank speed to turn the boat parallel to the track of the oncoming torpedo. A second glowing green line boiled up along the starboard side. According to Summers' patrol report:

> The night was clear and I'm sure that if there had been a submarine on the surface we could have seen it. As it turned out, I feel certain that a submerged enemy submarine had fired at us and his misses were due merely to the fact that we were zigzagging, for which I am now very thankful.

Pampanito submerged and tried to pick up the sound of the attacker's screws. Nothing was heard. At 2300 hours Summers received orders to remain in the area until the night of June 27 to intercept the remnants of a crippled enemy task force returning from the Battle of the Philippine Sea. *Whale* (SS-239), *Grouper* (SS-214), and *Batfish* (SS-310) also patrolled this area, but no contacts were made.

A frequent problem during this time was enemy shore-based radar. Each evening interference was briefly seen on *Pampanito*'s radar screen as radar installations ashore swept the coastal waters. When the radar interference was constant, they knew the Japanese were focusing on them. On such occasions, Summers submerged the boat to keep her position unknown.

This second war patrol was especially frustrating. Everyone on board knew they were in a "hot" area for enemy shipping. Yet none showed. For example, the entire morning of June 24 was spent submerging, first because of sampans and patrol craft, then a Zero flew over, forcing them down and finally a twin-engined "Betty" bomber did

At 0350 the officer of the deck, the navigator, and one of the lookouts sighted the phosphorescent wake of a torpedo crossing Pampanito*'s bow.*

DIVING

"Diving of the sub was always conducted under emergency or 'Crash Dive' conditions. By that I mean as soon as the officer of the deck ordered dive and hit the diving alarm, the chief petty officer on the diving manifold, in the control room, opened all the main ballast tank vents and the sub started down as the tanks filled with water. The engine room crew shut down the diesel engines and the electricians in the maneuvering room shifted propulsion to the sub's batteries. As soon as the engines were stopped, the CPO [Chief Petty Officer] operating the diving manifold would close the main induction valve to prevent water from flooding into the air induction lines. As the sub headed down, personnel on the bridge would come below through the conning tower hatch. There were normally about five men on the bridge: the OOD [Officer of the Deck], quartermaster and three lookouts. They had about thirty seconds to get through the conning tower hatch if we were making full speed on the surface. Our speed influenced the diving time. The slower our speed the longer it took to dive. The conning tower hatch was closed by the quartermaster as soon as the bridge was clear. The lookouts manned the bow and stern diving planes and the OOD acted as diving officer in control of the dive. Submerging a submarine had to be a well-coordinated operation conducted with precise timing. We had many opportunities to perfect the technique."

Woodrow Weaver

the same. Summers' chagrin was evident in his log, "This has been a hectic day — and we still haven't seen any traffic moving up and down the coast."

When convoys were seen, other difficulties hampered their success. Several potential targets were sighted including a destroyer and a seven-ship convoy, but each time *Pampanito* tried to position herself for an attack, she either had to dodge patrol craft or found that the pull of strong easterly currents threw her off. Matters were further complicated when both periscopes began fogging, and there was no nitrogen gas left aboard to dry them out.

It wasn't frustrating for everyone. Spencer Stimler, radio technician 2/c: "The excitement came when we were at battle stations.

Mostly that was at night since most of our attacks took place at night. We did spend a lot of time tracking the enemy and I was on radar when that took place. We would be secured from battle stations while tracking, but standing radar watch put me right in the center of the activity. It was exciting to be involved from the first contact until we fired the torpedoes."

By the night of July 5, *Pampanito* had moved eastward, through the seven mile wide channel between the islands of Nii Shima and Kozu Shima. The sky cleared and a moonlit night revealed an unobstructed view of both islands. Summers then reversed course and headed westward between the two islands to be nearer the coast. Just after dawn the next morning a trawler was sighted and avoided. It was too small to justify the expense of a torpedo.

Around 0730 a "Betty" bomber flew by and additional trawlers were seen patrolling the area. Just after noon a three ship convoy was sighted. After checking the recognition publication it was decided the two largest ships were a Toyokawa Maru-class, rated at 5,100 tons and a Kenyo Maru-class, rated at 6,100 tons. There was also a tanker they were unable to identify. Escorted by an Otori-class gunboat, a second gunboat, a trawler and an air cover of three amphibious zeroes, the convoy made a challenging target. It was a calm afternoon with glassy seas making an undetected approach all the more difficult. The convoy's base course was 90 degrees. *Pampanito* remained ahead and slightly south of the projected track. Summers was able to get off a three-torpedo spread from the stern tubes at the leading target. One torpedo hit. The ensuing depth charge attack drove *Pampanito* deep so the results of the attack could not be confirmed.

Depth charging was a new experience to Spencer Stimler. "My first thought when I heard my first depth charge was that the 7/8" pressure hull sounded more like being inside a tin can. It didn't give me a great feeling of security."

It was also Motor Machinist's Mate 3/c Harry Bowring's initial patrol on *Pampanito*. "One of the first things that would happen when we were being depth charged was 'silent running.' This meant all electricity was ceased and everything in the boat was run by hand hydraulics. I would feel tense but was never actually afraid that I would die. I put my life in the hands of the Lord and knew that everything would be okay. I

Just after dawn the next morning a trawler was sighted and avoided. It was too small to justify the expense of a torpedo.

TRIM

Keeping the boat in trim or level was a constant problem as her weight was continually changing with the use of fuel and the shifting of weight from one place to another. Even the location of the crew could affect a submarine's trim. Firing torpedoes created another trim problem. The loss of the weight of the torpedo had to be compensated for immediately, or the bow (if the torpedo was fired from the forward torpedo room) would rise and the stern fall. Harry Bowring, motor machinist's mate 2/c: "My duties for battle stations were: I was in charge of the trim manifold in the control room. I would let water in and out of the trim manifold to keep the boat level/balanced. When a torpedo was discharged this would reduce the weight of the boat and I would have to add more water to the trim manifold to prevent the boat from becoming unbalanced or from broaching."

The hull opening indicator panel shows whether hull openings such as doors, hatches, valves, vents, etc. are open (green light) or closed (red light). A full panel of green lights meant it was safe to dive. Author.

definitely felt a big sigh of relief, however, when we would hear them going away from the sub."

Earl Watkins, motor machinist's mate 2/c: "It was very scary. To say I wasn't scared would be a lie. It was like paying your dues after you sank some ships."

In the patrol log Summers stated:

1340 - First of eleven depth charges; all big and set shallow but not close. This was the most half hearted depth charging I have ever witnessed, mainly

due, I believe, to the fact that the enemy had no idea where we were (because we had fired Mark 18's [electric torpedoes which left no wake]) and could not hear or pick us up in the shallow water to seaward of the attack because of the sharp temperature gradient.

Woodrow Weaver: "We were carrying sixteen Mark 14 steam torpedoes in the forward torpedo room and eight Mark 18 electric torpedoes in the after room. The steam torpedoes had the advantage of longer range, but left a detectable wake when fired. The electric torpedoes, which left no wake, were preferred by our CO because of the added security when firing from a submerged position."

The hydrophone crew heard the target's screws stop and the sound of a ship breaking up. A little later, periscope observation showed that the leading ship was dead in the water, apparently hit by the second or third torpedo which ran under the escort. The remainder of the convoy had such close air cover that Summers decided against further action. He submerged and eased away from the area at a depth of 250 feet.

Later that night and back on the surface, a lookout reported a periscope less than a mile to port. A few minutes later, radar showed a plane closing in. In fact, that night the lookouts had the first night sighting of an enemy patrol airplane. They were frequent during daylight hours but this was the first at night. Summers believed they were searching for *Pampanito* because of the attack.

Pampanito dove and continued farther east and south to another part of her assigned patrol area. While patrolling on the surface west of the island of Hachijo Shima with a partial moon silhouetting her on July 16 at 0340 a torpedo wake was sighted moving toward her port beam. She immediately came left to parallel the track of the torpedo. It was estimated later that the weapon crossed *Pampanito's* bow as she turned, missing her by a mere three to five yards. A second torpedo followed close on the heels of the first. Summers again attributed the miss to his continuous use of a zig-zag course when surfaced.

That same day Summers received a report of an enemy convoy approaching and, although scheduled to depart, spent an extra day searching; however, a U.S. submarine was the only vessel sighted. Diminishing fuel supplies forced *Pampanito* to leave the area and return to Midway.

The Japanese midget submarine (shown is the Type C) was 86 ft. long and carried a crew of five. It was armed with two torpedoes. Later in the war the torpedoes were replaced with explosive charges and the boat became a suicide craft. Conway Maritime Press.

Woodrow Weaver: "Enemy shipping was non-existent and it turned out to be a disappointing patrol."

Arriving at Midway on July 23, *Pampanito* again met with the sub tender *Proteus* for repairs and refit. Once again, a brass band welcomed their arrival. Sacks of mail and crates of fresh fruit and vegetables lined the pier.

Elmer Smith, torpedoman 2/c: "My most memorable experience on the *Pampanito* was coming into port after my first patrol [he joined at the beginning of the second war patrol] with the band on the dock — all the accumulated mail and the feeling of relief."

Woodrow Weaver: "We had to off load our torpedoes before turning the boat over to the relief crew. This proved to be physically demanding. I did not realize how much the long days of submerged operations had taken out of us. We would unload one torpedo then pause for a rest. After the job was completed we turned everything over to the relief crew and headed for the rest camp.

Listening to Summers' report of the second war patrol Admiral Lockwood, Commander of the Submarine Force Pacific, speculated that the torpedoes fired at *Pampanito* may have come from a midget Japanese submarine. He also made note of the increase in use of land-based radar by the enemy.

Rather than return to the Royal Hawaiian at Honolulu, *Pampanito*'s crew was slated for rest and recreation at Midway. The barracks-like structures in the rest camp were primitive. Woodrow Weaver: "One of the first things I wanted was a good shower. I grabbed a towel and soap and headed for the shower bath. When I turned the water on I received a rude shock. The showers were supplied with salt water! I jumped out of the shower stall and never attempted another while we were at Midway. Fresh water was a scarce item."

"I did not realize how much the long days of submerged operations had taken out of us. We would unload one torpedo then pause for a rest."

Woodrow Weaver

Unwinding at Midway, the crew relaxes while Pampanito *is prepared for her next patrol. San Francisco Maritime National Park Association.*

The only recreation available on Midway was "swimming, picnics, fighting and gambling." Those assigned to the island were frustrated by their confined duty and rigged up gambling casinos in the mess halls after working hours. Usually the games were dice and poker. Most of the *Pampanito* crew avoided the casinos. Those running them were too good at what they were doing for the average submariner to have a sporting chance.

Of course, there was always drinking to pass the time. Spencer Stimler: "The enlisted men had all the beer they could drink, for free, at the beer hall when it was open. The officers were allotted hard liquor. One time, two of the enlisted men, Herber and Yagemann, sneaked into the officers' quarters and swiped a bottle of bourbon from Lt. Swain. They drank it all themselves and were in the crew's quarters feeling no

pain when Mr. Swain appeared at the door. He didn't come in but said, 'Yagemann and Herber, I want to talk to you.'

"Yagemann quickly replied, 'Honest, Mr. Swain, we didn't steal your whiskey.'

"This broke everybody up including Lt. Swain, who left trying not to laugh too hard."

Pampanito was refitted and prepared for her third patrol.

6

THE THIRD WAR PATROL
17 August - 28 September 1944

After more than three weeks on Midway, the crew was almost eager for the next patrol. The antics of the gooney birds soon lost their attraction and other than card games, drinking and reading, there was little to do.

While the men relaxed, *Pampanito* was tended by USS *Proteus* (AS-19) whose crew provided repairs and supplies. Improvements included the installation of a radio key in the SJ radar circuit, a surface search device that allowed the radar to be used for communications. Charging equipment was built into the forward torpedo room so that Mark 18 electric torpedoes could be fired from the six forward tubes. She already had this installation in the after torpedo room. Routine maintenance and repairs included replacing the brushes in all four of the 1600-horsepower electric main propulsion motors. The gaskets were replaced on the conning tower hatch, main air induction valve, and the newly converted Fuel Ballast Tank No. 4A. Then final preparations were made for getting underway: provisions, fuel,

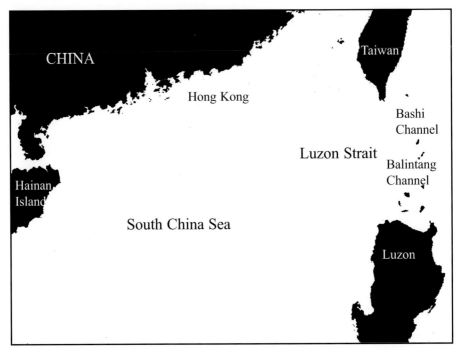

The third war patrol began in Bashi Channel, covering the area from there down to Luzon, then across to the coastal waters east of Hainan Island and back through Balintang Channel toward Saipan.

ammunition, and torpedoes were loaded aboard. On August 17, 1944 USS *Pampanito* was ready for sea.

Woodrow Weaver, torpedoman 1/c: "Our C.O. liked the performance of the electric torpedoes and had requested a full complement. They were a bit more work for the torpedomen. We had to pull the torpedoes part way out of the tubes to charge their batteries. The batteries had to have a re-charge about every four or five days to keep them fully charged."

Departing Midway under the command of Paul E. Summers, newly promoted to full commander, *Pampanito* headed for the Luzon Strait north of the Philippine Islands. This area was code named "Convoy College" because of the large number of Japanese ships that converged there as they traveled north to Japan.

THE WOLF PACK

Admiral Dönitz of the German navy experimented with the concept while a junior officer in World War I. Where a single sub could be avoided by a convoy or located and sunk by its escorts, wolf packs were much more difficult to deal with. Submarines could attack from several directions simultaneously, confusing both targets and escorts. If escorts focused on one submarine, the others could finish off the convoy or, in some cases, attack the attackers. Dönitz established wolf packs of four and five boats. German wolf packs were the scourge of Allied shipping in the North Atlantic during World War II.

Wolf packs became more common in the Pacific as Japanese convoys became better organized and protected. The U.S. Navy seldom used more than three boats but frequently instructed one wolfpack to back up another, effectively creating a group of six or more boats working together. The results were devastating to Japan.

Unlike her first two patrols when she operated alone, *Pampanito* traveled as part of a wolf pack which included USS *Growler* (SS-215), and USS *Sealion* (SS-315).

Skippers used their radios sparingly to avoid detection by any Japanese that might be tuned in to their frequency. They preferred rendezvousing regularly at pre-selected times and communicating by signal lights with Morse code or, if weather permitted, shouting through megaphones. This pack, nicknamed "Ben's Busters" after tactical leader Cdr. T.B. "Ben" Oakley, included Oakley in *Growler* (SS-215), Second

USS Growler *(SS-215) as she appeared on February 21, 1942 at Groton, Connecticut.* National Archives.

The first Sealion *(SS-195) was severely damaged in the Japanese attack on Cavite on December 8, 1941. Considered beyond repair, she was destroyed on December 25.*

Senior Officer Cdr. Eli T. Reich, in *Sealion* (SS-315), and Summers in *Pampanito*.

En route to the patrol area the three boats exchanged recognition signals and tested communications via VHF radio. On August 19, Summers noted in his patrol report that he was having difficulty communicating with *Growler* when the range exceeded 8,000 yards. As this was just a little less than four nautical miles, he doubted they would be able to communicate during any kind of coordinated attack.

When "Ben's Busters" attacked a Japanese convoy in Bashi Channel off the southern tip of Formosa on August 30, they operated with another wolf pack, "Ed's Eradicators." This group included tactical commander Capt. Edwin Swineburne in USS *Barb* (SS-220) which was skippered by Cdr. Eugene Fluckey, and Cdr. Charles Loughlin in *Queenfish* (SS-393). The attack was frustrating to *Pampanito*. While the two wolf packs attacked the convoy, sinking seven ships and damaging others, *Pampanito* was just below the horizon, her lookouts reporting distant explosions and the glow of a burning ship brightening the dark sky. This was followed by distant depth charges. Poor communications had placed the boat off the intended track of the convoy. No contact report was received from the two attacking wolf packs, and Summers searched in vain for the remnants of the scattered convoy.

During the next few days *Pampanito* developed a serious mechanical problem. A loud air squeal was heard forward during a dive, and the diving officer reported 2,000 pounds of water in the forward trim tank.

Woodrow Weaver: "The leak presented no immediate danger except it upset the trim of the boat in diving operations. The sub would get heavy forward and water would have to be pumped to sea to correct the trim."

The water could be compensated for, but the noise would give the boat away when attacking the enemy. It had to be repaired. The exact location of the noise couldn't be determined because it was internal. Locating the leak meant putting someone inside the tank while the sub dove. On the night of September 4, Lt. Howard Fulton and Motor Machinist E.W. Stockslader, volunteered for the dangerous task.

While the two wolf packs attacked the convoy, sinking seven ships and damaging others, Pampanito *was just below the horizon, her lookouts reporting distant explosions and the glow of a burning ship brightening the dark sky.*

Woodrow Weaver: "Two men went topside at night, removed the manhole cover from the forward trim tank and then went down inside. The manhole cover was then replaced and we submerged with the men in the tank."

A signal system was set up. *Pampanito* dove to sixty feet. Nothing showed. Summers took her deeper, to 200 feet, before the leak was finally located. After surfacing, the manhole was opened and the men released from the tank. They reported that the seal around the operating rod to torpedo tube No. 5 leaked where it passed through the forward bulkhead of the tank. This was a difficult area to reach and blueprints were studied for two days before a workable solution was developed.

Pampanito surfaced at night to repair the leak. Tony Hauptman, first class gunners' mate, volunteered to do the work. Using a shallow water diving apparatus he worked his way below the waterline and under the superstructure. Hauptman made repeated dives and fixed the noisy leak although a specially made wrench had to be devised to secure the last bolt tightly. *Pampanito* was again able to maneuver silently and the war patrol continued without having to turn back to Midway for repair.

Woodrow Weaver: "All this was accomplished at great risk for those directly involved. If we had been detected by the enemy, the skipper would have been forced to dive and abandon the men topside. They knew this, yet volunteered for the job."

Pete Summers celebrated his thirty-first birthday at sea on September 6, 1944, the same day an enemy convoy left Singapore bound through "Convoy College" to Japan. The convoy carried bauxite, needed to produce aluminum, rubber and oil. It also carried over two thousand British and Australian prisoners of war being transported from Southeast Asia.

These men were part of the workforce that completed the Burma-Thailand railroad. This infamous "Railway of Death," as it became known, was used by the Japanese to move troops and supplies 250 miles through the mountainous jungles of Thailand and Burma connecting with other lines running through Southeast Asia and out to the South China Sea. The railway was built at a huge cost in human life. An estimated

"If we had been detected by the enemy, the skipper would have been forced to dive and abandon the men topside. They knew this, yet volunteered for the job."

Woodrow Weaver

12,000 British, Australian, and many times that number of Asian prisoners died from jungle diseases, lack of medical care, starvation, abuse and overwork.[1]

The fittest of the railway survivors, known as the "Japan Party," were being relocated to work as forced labor in the copper mines of Japan.

Imprisoned in the bowels of the Japanese ships, the POWs were worried about the likelihood of being torpedoed en route by American submarines and made what preparations they could. Some formed teams and planned escape routes off the ship; others stockpiled their meager rations or tested the effects of drinking small amounts of sea water.

K.C. Renton, POW: "On the fatal day of the 4th Sep., 1944 we boarded a Jap convoy bound for Japan. Little hope of reaching there but miracles do happen (but not this time). There was eleven ships in the convoy. There was thirteen hundred prisoners on the ship I was on and another."

FRUPAC, the U.S. Fleet Radio Unit PACific, intercepted and decoded a Japanese message detailing the course and estimated noon positions of the convoy along the route to Japan. On the night of September 9, the "Busters" received an Ultra message to rendezvous on September 11 and intercept the convoy. Later that night, the "Eradicators" were ordered to back up the Busters and move in on the convoy, as well. *Growler,* first to arrive at the meeting point on the night of the 11th, found light overcast and calm seas with rain on the horizon. *Sealion* surfaced nearby around 2000 hours, having just returned from Saipan where her torpedoes, fired during the August 30th attack, were replaced. *Pampanito* moved in an hour-and-a-half later. The boats exchanged recognition signals with the SJ radar and moved within 100 yards of *Growler* to receive vocal instructions for the attack. The wolf pack then took up positions across the intended track of the approaching convoy.

At 0130 on the morning of September 12, *Pampanito's* George Moffett, radio technician 2/c, picked up several pips on the screen at a range of over fifteen miles. A few minutes later, a contact report was received from *Growler,* but the message was garbled. Summers ordered

---

[1] Part of this story was told in the famous book and movie, "The Bridge on the River Kwai."

flank speed to maneuver ahead of the convoy and into attack position. *Growler* approached from the west and fired on the ships, causing the convoy's escorts to fan out in all directions. *Growler*'s attack was a first and last in U.S. submarine history.

Growler was seen on radar by the Japanese escort *Hirado* as she moved in to attack. The escort charged the sub. Instead of diving the boat and taking evasive measures *Growler* faced the oncoming escort bow to bow on the surface, firing three torpedoes at the vessel from a range of just over 1,000 yards. The first torpedo hit, causing a violent explosion. The escort, listing badly, charged ahead, coming so close that Oakley felt the heat from the burning ship. *Hirado* finally went under, sinking only 200 yards from *Growler*. *Growler* escaped and went on to damage two other ships before moving out of range to reload her torpedo tubes.

K.C. Renton: "On the morning of the twelfth the fireworks started, one of the escorts went to the bottom."

A bright quarter moon had risen and, at 0230, Summers moved to the dark side of the scattered convoy. *Sealion* pulled back to repair a jammed automatic gyro setter. *Growler* lost the track of the convoy temporarily, and "Ed's Eradicators," *Queenfish* and *Barb,* had not received the contact reports concerning the battle and were eighty miles to the north. *Pampanito* and *Sealion* tracked the convoy for the remainder of the night, both boats moving into attack range just before dawn.

Summers carefully set up his approach, waiting for the enemy ships to come within range. As he prepared to fire from a perfect position, *Pampanito* was jolted by a series of violent explosions. *Sealion,* to the west, had fired two salvos of three torpedoes each at the convoy. Once again, *Pampanito* was cheated of her chance. The first salvo scored two hits on the 8,400 ton naval transport *Nankai Maru*, which erupted into flames so bright they illuminated the second target, the transport *Rakuyo Maru*.

Rakuyo Maru was a 477-foot Japanese-built passenger-cargo vessel carrying a load of raw rubber and, unknown to the crews of the submarines, over 1,300 Allied prisoners of war. Two of *Sealion*'s torpedoes hit the POW ship, one amidships and one in the bow. It took twelve hours for *Rakuyo Maru* to sink. Their Japanese guards left the ship immediately after the attack, taking most of the lifeboats. The surviving

Unknown to the crews of the submarines, Rakuyo Maru *carried over 1,300 Allied prisoners of war. Two of* Sealion's *torpedoes hit the POW ship, one amidships and one in the bow.*

POWs were left on their own to make rafts and search the doomed ship for food and water.

K.C. Renton: "Later in the morning, less than two hours, our ship received two torpedoes. There seemed to be ships ablaze everywhere. I must say this about the lads. There was no panic and, by the way, our ship did not catch alight which was a great thing. She finally sank that evening. Well, the Japs on the boat beat it rowing boats and I found my self in the water."

Sealion went deep to avoid depth charging. *Growler* and *Pampanito* tracked the convoy as it zigzagged radically to avoid further attack. *Growler* caught up with and sank another Japanese escort, the destroyer *Shikinami*. The POWs, who were now in the water clinging to wreckage, had mixed feelings as the warship instantly sank. Some cheered another score against their captors; others saw all chances of rescue sink with that ship. Tragically, many survivors of the initial attack were killed or badly wounded by shock waves caused by the explosions of *Shikinami*'s sinking and the following depth charge attack on *Growler*.

K.C. Renton: "The only queer sensation was the depth charges exploding but were too far away to do damage. By the end of the day the Japs were picked up by two gun boats and they left us to perish, which we fully expected."

Pampanito again picked up the convoy on high periscope at noon the next day, and tracked it westward. Just after dark, Summers moved in for a surface attack.

Woodrow Weaver: "We had been at battle stations for an hour or more when the *Pampanito* got into attack position. In the forward torpedo room, we received the order to 'Make ready forward tubes for firing.' As the tubes were flooded with water, the torpedo in No. 4 tube slid forward, the motor started and we had a hot run in the tube."

Summers had to pull back again.

Woodrow Weaver: "The skipper was very calm about it and ordered No. 4 tube secured. The running torpedo caused a bit of excitement among my reload crew. They were mostly seamen, not trained in torpedoes, and they could envision the torpedo warhead exploding and blowing the bow off the submarine. We torpedomen knew there was no danger as torpedoes were designed to run a short distance before the warhead explosive device could be activated.

The POWs, who were now in the water clinging to wreckage, had mixed feelings as the warship instantly sank. Some cheered another score against their captors; others saw all chances of rescue sink with that ship.

"My station was on the blow and vent manifold just aft of the tubes. My assistant, Jim Behney, was operating the tube interlocks which had to be aligned to open the outer doors. He was positioned between the tubes. Just ahead of Jim, Little Joe Austin was sitting on a wooden stool operating the equipment which transmitted gyro setting information from the torpedo data computer in the conning tower. When the torpedo started to run, I looked around just in time to see my reload crew disappearing through the watertight door into the next compartment, which was the forward battery room. There was no significant danger to us. The worst part was the loss of one of our offensive weapons.

"The captain continued his approach and then ordered 'Open outer doors on forward tubes.' About this time the reload crew, satisfied that the torpedo was not going to explode, came back into the compartment."

A few minutes later the boat was once again in position. From the War Patrol log::

> 2240 Fired five torpedoes forward; three at large transport and two at large AK
> … Swung hard right and at
> 2243 Fired four stern tubes; two at each of the two AK's in the farthest column. Saw three hits in large AP, two hits in large AK (Targets no. 1 and 2) and one hit in AK (farthest column) heard and timed, hit in fourth AK (leading ship in farthest column) … In all, seven hits out of nine torpedoes. From the bridge we watched both the large AP and the large AK (the one with two hits) sink within the next ten minutes, and saw the after deck house of the third ship, on which we saw one hit, go up into the air with the ship smoking heavily. The fourth ship could not be observed … because of much smoke and haze in that direction. A short interval after the seven hits, the escorts started dropping depth charges at random, but for once we didn't mind.

Pampanito had sunk a 524-foot transport *Kachidoki Maru,* a captured American vessel built in New Jersey in 1921. First owned by United States Lines, and later the Dollar Line, she had originally been named *Wolverine State.* After being sold to American President Lines (which succeeded Dollar Line), she was renamed *President Harrison.* When captured off the China coast by the Japanese, she was given the

This drawing by Gunner's Mate Tony Hauptman shows the Kachidoki Maru *at the moment of torpedo impact. San Francisco Maritime National Park Association.*

name *Kachidoki Maru.* Like the *Rakuyo Maru,* the ship was carrying raw materials to Japan. Also aboard were 900 Allied POWs.

Following the attack, *Pampanito* pulled away to eject the hot run torpedo and reload all tubes. An hour later, in another attack, Summers missed with three shots fired at a destroyer escort. At that time he also saw two small ships, one of which had stopped, apparently to pick up survivors of the earlier attack. He decided they were too small to waste time and a torpedo on, and moved on to rejoin the pack on the following night. No immediate attempt was made to track down the remaining stragglers from the convoy.

The U.S. wolf pack rendezvoused the night of September 13th. *Growler* moved south while *Sealion* and *Pampanito* spent the next day

Pampanito *had sunk a 524-foot transport,* Kachidoki Maru *... the ship was carrying raw materials and 900 Allied POWs to Japan.*

Here, Tony Hauptman shows Pampanito *pulling away to reload with the burning* Kachidoki Maru *in the background. San Francisco Maritime National Park Association.*

looking in vain for the rest of the convoy, then headed east toward the area of the September 12th attack on *Rakuyo Maru*. After diving to avoid a plane late in the afternoon of the 15th, *Pampanito* surfaced amid a floating field of debris and wreckage.

Woodrow Weaver: "We were steaming on the surface when one of the lookouts sighted a man on a raft. Our CO thought it was a stranded Japanese sailor and decided to take him prisoner. When we pulled alongside the raft, the man hailed us in English and asked to be picked up."

The first man pick up was Frank Farmer.

K.C. Renton: "For three nights and four days I was afloat on the open sea, no water and no food, covered in oil and only a singlet on. We were many miles from land and it looked like the end. There was about a dozen of us on four or five rafts drifting about wherever the current liked to take us. On the fourth day we all began to go a bit dippy, some more than others, and in our little party two threw themselves over. They had been drinking sea water that afternoon.

The President Harrison *(later* Kachidoki Maru*) as she appeared while operating for Dollar Lines. American President Lines*

"Between four and five that wonderful thing happened. A submarine was making straight for us but we did not know who it belonged to. My eyes were paining with oil and I could not see clearly but when it was right opposite, I saw a couple of men with machine guns pointing them at us. I did not care because it would have been a quicker way out and believe me, they looked tough. But instead of lead we got a rope and were taken aboard. Can you imagine the shock. We got water, tomato soup and crackers and the Lord only knows what for our first dinner, something we never had for 2½ years and since then we lived like lords. There was seventy-three survivors taken aboard."

1605   A bridge lookout sighted some men on a raft, so stood by small arms, and closed to investigate.

1634   The men were covered with oil and filth and we could not make them out. They were shouting but we couldn't understand what they were

At great risk to their own lives, many of the crew went over the side to help the POWs on board. San Francisco Maritime National Park Association.

"I saw a couple of men with machine guns pointing them at us. I did not care because it would have been a quicker way out and believe me, they looked tough."

K.C. Renton

saying, except made out words "Pick us up, please.' Called rescue party on deck and took them off the raft. There were about fifteen (15) British and Australian Prisoner of War survivors on this raft from a ship sunk the night of 11-12 September, 1944. We learned they were enroute from Singapore to Formosa and that there were over thirteen hundred on the sunken ship.

The crew of *Pampanito* spent the next four hours rescuing as many survivors as could be found. Under the direction of torpedo officer Lt. Ted Swain, volunteer teams were formed to get the almost helpless men aboard. Some of *Pampanito's* crew dove into the water with lines to attach to the rafts so they could be brought in close enough for others on deck and on the saddle tanks to carefully lift the men aboard. Among those crew members who swam out to rescue the former POWs, leaving the relative safety of the sub and risking being left behind if the boat had to dive, were Bob Bennett, Andrew Currier, Bill Yagemann, Gordon Hopper, Jim Behney, and Tony Hauptman.

Bill Fisk, engineman 2/c: "I did a lot of the swimming. I was one of the first topside. They passed the word, they asked for qualified swimmers. Being from L.A. I easily qualified. By the time it was all over, numerous people were in the water."

It was a tense and emotional time as the shocked crew worked to save as many of the oil soaked survivors as possible. During the rescue many of the crew came topside to help. If a Japanese plane attacked at that time they would have been left on deck as *Pampanito* dove to avoid attack.

As the POWs were brought alongside, others in the crew prepared to bring them aboard. San Francisco Maritime National Park Association.

Adrift for several days, the POWs were covered with oil and suffering from exposure and dehydration as well as the privation and tropical diseases they contracted in captivity. San Francisco Maritime National Park Association.

And for a moment, they thought that was exactly what was happening. Clarence Williams, electrician's mate 3/c: "I was lookout when we were rescuing the POWs. I spotted what I thought was a flight of planes. It was only when they turned and I thought they were diving on us, I saw that it was a flock of birds."

Capt. Summers recorded: "Fortunately one of the "planes" was seen to flap its wings, proving the formation to be large birds gliding in perfect order."

During the rescue many of the crew came topside to help. If a Japanese plane attacked at that time they would have been left on deck as Pampanito *dove to avoid attack.*

Bill Fisk: "People don't understand what a risk that was, because we were only [about two hundred] miles off the Chinese mainland and the Japanese patrolled frequently. If they had caught us with hatches open, it would have been the end. It would have meant the loss of the boat. If a Jap sub had come along it would have been like shooting fish in a barrel."

Gently, as much of the oil and grime as possible was removed before sending the survivors below. One, lower right, even managed a weak smile of gratitude. San Francisco Maritime National Park Association.

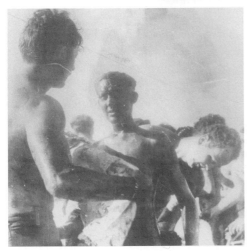

Frank Farmer, POW: "Had aircraft approached, the enemy coast was not that far away, Capt. Summers would have had to make a terrible decision to crash dive and leave some of his crew with us — possibly to die."

Clarence Smith: "We were picking up survivors, volunteers going into the water and help up there and one thing and another. I was stationed at the bottom of the hatch, because I was the biggest man aboard ship, to catch them coming down.

"That was the only time I ever wore a sidearm, on that deck watch, because we didn't know what we were getting into. So we put a .45 on. Because if we'd of gotten a hold of some Nips or something like that, we don't know what the reaction would have been if they come down. But the word soon came down, 'Someone out there in the water hollered, that's a Yank.'

"But to see those fellas come aboard and that ungodly mess of muck and grease and the condition they were in, tropical sores and everything of that kind."

Harry Bowring, motor machinist's mate 2/c: "I was in the engine room and the survivors started coming down the hatch. We all helped clean them up, gave them clothes, and gave them our bunks."

These men were survivors of *Rakuyo Maru,* sunk earlier by *Sealion.* After four days of drifting on makeshift rafts they were in extremely bad shape. Most were covered with oil from the sunken tanker, and had long since used up what little food and water they had with them. Slowly, the story of what happened was told by the survivors brought aboard *Pampanito.* Summers radioed *Sealion,* and Reich also moved in to pick up survivors.

Again from the patrol reports:

1634 As the men were received on board, we stripped them and removed most of the heavy coating of oil and muck. We cleared the after torpedo room and passed them below as quickly as possible. Gave all men a piece of cloth moistened with water to suck on. All of them were exhausted after four days on the raft and three years imprisonment. Many had lashed themselves to their makeshift rafts, which were slick with grease; and had nothing but lifebelts with them. All showed signs of pellagra, beriberi, malaria, immersion, salt water sores, ringworm, etc. All were very

"If a Jap sub had come along it would have been like shooting fish in a barrel."

Bill Fisk

thin and showed the results of under nourishment. Some were in very bad shape … A pitiful sight none of us will ever forget. All hands turned to with a will and the men were cared for as rapidly as possible.

1701 Sent message to *Sealion* for help.

1712 Picked up a second raft with about nine men aboard.

1721 Picked up another six men.

1730 Rescued another six men.

1753 Picked up about eleven men.

1824 … about six men.

1832 … about five men.

1957 Light fading rapidly as we picked up a single survivor.

2005 Completely dark as we took aboard the last group of about ten men. Had made a thorough search of our vicinity with high periscope and kept the true bearings of all rafts sighted. Felt we had everyone in sight and knew we had all we could care for if not more. When finally we obtained an exact count, the number of survivors on board was 73. These together with 79 members of our crew plus 10 officers make us a little cramped for living space.

2015 Made final search and finding no one else set course for Saipan at four engine speed.

Frank Farmer, POW: "I think you must realize that the hopes and fears of our years of captivity were all realized on that day. Of course, for others, it was the worst. But no time while in the water or afterwards did I hear any words of censure. Those that died at least had the consolation of knowing that they died free men. And also having witnessed the results of that attack on the convoy they knew that the cause for which they had lived and fought and died would prevail."

Manuel Mendez, torpedoman 3/c: "It turned out to be a thing of joy to then rescue some seventy-three Allied service men who had been Japanese prisoners of war since the fall of Singapore."

Woodrow Weaver: "They were in bad physical condition. They were suffering from dehydration as well as all sorts of diseases contracted in the Burma jungle. They had malaria, dysentery, ringworm and other ailments. They were oil-soaked and horribly sunburned from exposure for better than two days. We had our hands full cleaning them up and attending to their needs."

"Those that died at least had the consolation of knowing that they died free men."

Frank Farmer

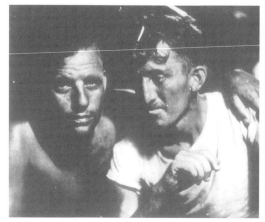

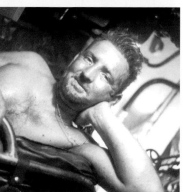

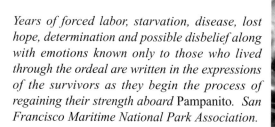

Years of forced labor, starvation, disease, lost hope, determination and possible disbelief along with emotions known only to those who lived through the ordeal are written in the expressions of the survivors as they begin the process of regaining their strength aboard Pampanito. *San Francisco Maritime National Park Association.*

During the five-day trip to Saipan, the nearest Allied port, the survivors were berthed in the crew's quarters amidships and on the empty torpedo skids and bunks in the after torpedo room.

Bill Fisk: "We had ninety men on board in crew and we took on seventy-three POWs. They were everywhere. The sick ones they put in bunks, and those that weren't so bad off, would kind of hot bunk. They were in all the compartments, in bunks everywhere, in skids and so on. They had them in every compartment, some of them even slept in the engine room."

Harry Bowring: "We would just doze off wherever we could until we got to port with the survivors. We doubled the amount of the personnel with the survivors. They were in rough shape and we all willingly gave them whatever they needed."

Some of the survivors were critically ill and in need of medical attention. The only man on board with training in medicine was Pharmacist Mate First Class Maurice L. Demers. With the help of crew members who fed the men and donated clothing, Demers worked around the clock. Of the survivors, one of the British POWs, John Campbell, was the most seriously ill. Demers worked continually to save the delirious Campbell, but he died the next day, September 16.

Charles A. McGuire, yeoman 1/c: "We lost one fella in there, down in the crew's quarters. He was in the after bunk on the port side, top bunk. We had canvas and sewed him up in a bag and put in two gun rounds and put him over the side."

Harry Bowring: "We gave them a weight to attach for the burial at sea. We gave them a spare connecting rod that we had in the engine room."

John Campbell was buried at sea following a somber ceremony during which Paul Pappas read a heartfelt prayer.

Charles A. McGuire: "Pop Pappas was on the deckside service for him, out there. That was one of the men out of the crew instead of one of their own. They didn't expect to be treated that way."

At one point, as Demers tried to get a few hours sleep, several of the survivors took a turn for the worse, and he was awakened. Demers continued tending the survivors until he came dangerously close to total exhaustion. Campbell was the only casualty.

In a letter written after the war Demers said "… as I examined and treated each one I could feel a deep sense of gratitude, their faces were expressionless and only a few could move their lips to whisper a faint 'thanks.' It was quite gratifying to see the happy expressions on their faces when they left the ship."

Bill Fisk: "One of the guys slept in the forward engine room, and I kind of took care of him with soft boiled eggs and so on. When he left the ship he gave each one of us three diamonds, three to a guy named Grady and three to a guy named Smith."

Before leaving for Saipan, Summers sent off a message to Pearl Harbor explaining the situation and requested that more subs be brought in to continue the rescue. *Queenfish* and *Barb,* the only other boats in the area, were ordered in as soon as possible. They were 450 miles west in

"*… as I examined and treated each one I could feel a deep sense of gratitude, their faces were expressionless and only a few could move their lips to whisper a faint 'thanks.'*"
Maurice L. Demers

pursuit of a convoy, but on receiving the new orders they immediately headed full speed to the rescue area. During the night of September 16th they encountered a convoy of large tankers and, among the escorts, a small aircraft carrier. The subs attacked the convoy and *Barb* quickly sank the carrier *Unyo* and an 11,000-ton tanker. They then continued on to the rescue area.

Queenfish and *Barb* arrived at 0530 on the 17th to begin their search for survivors among the floating debris. Just after 1300 they located several rafts and picked up the few men still alive. After a few hours a typhoon moved in, sealing the fate of those not already picked up. Before the storm hit, *Queenfish* found eighteen men, and *Barb* found fourteen. They rode out the storm, made a final search which produced no additional survivors and headed for Saipan.

Of the 1,318 POWs on the *Rakuyo Maru* sunk by *Sealion,* 159 were rescued by the four submarines: seventy-three on *Pampanito*, fifty-four on *Sealion,* and the thirty-two found by *Queenfish* and *Barb*. It was later learned that the Japanese rescued 136 for a total of 295 survivors. Of the 900 POWs on the *Kachidoki Maru* sunk by *Pampanito,* 520 were rescued by the Japanese making a total of 656 taken to prison camps in Japan. More than 500 of these men were released by American troops in August, 1945 at the close of the war.

Woodrow Weaver: "As soon as we could, the cooks provided food. The rescued prisoners were started off on soup and gradually introduced to solid food. The unfamiliar food caused most of them to have diarrhea. The after torpedo room is serviced by only one head that had to be discharged to sea after use. The poor guys were lining up to use the one head, and we had to have a man on watch to operate the discharge valves for them. The poor sailor on that watch had quite a job. As fast as he took care of one man, there was another ready to sit on the commode. In telling about this in later years, I have compared it to having sixty or more men in your hallway, all with diarrhea, wanting to use your bathroom."

On September 18th, as *Pampanito* traveled to Saipan, she was met by the USS *Case* (DD 370) and took aboard a pharmacist mate, medical supplies, and a doctor. Still, Maurice Demers, who had saved so many lives, continued to care for the former POWs. On the morning of

Of the 1,318 POWs on the Rakuyo Maru *sunk by* Sealion, *159 were rescued by the four submarines: seventy-three on* Pampanito, *fifty-four on* Sealion, *and the thirty-two found by* Queenfish *and* Barb.

the 20th, *Pampanito* was met by the USS *Dunlap* (DD-84) which escorted *Pampanito* into Tanapag Harbor, Saipan, where she docked alongside the submarine tender USS *Fulton* (AS-11). Fresh fruit and ice cream were brought aboard for the POWs as preparations were made for transferring them to the *Fulton.* The transfer was complete by 1100 that morning and *Pampanito's* crew bid farewell to the grateful and much improved former POWs.

The destroyer Case *(DD-370) approaches* Pampanito *as she nears Saipan, to put aboard a pharmisict's mate and medical supplies. San Francisco Maritime National Park Association.*

Bill Fisk: "They were only on there a few days. I don't think any sub could have gone any quicker from China to Saipan."

Charles A. McGuire: "To see those boys walk off this boat at Saipan was something."

Bill Fisk: "They were all really decent, good men."

Manuel Mendez: "Their expressions of gratitude upon leaving us in Saipan was thanks enough for us all."

K.C. Renton: "I don't know how to put my feelings into words but may God bless the captain and the crew for the wonderful job they did in saving our lives and looking after us. There is not a man that won't forget it. I now look forward to a rest and later going home to Ausie and joining some Batt. and start where I left off if time permits. I hope that a lot more of my comrades were picked up, but those who went, may they rest in peace."

Pampanito took on fuel and provisions and left for Hawaii at 1600 that afternoon, arriving for refit at Submarine Base, Pearl Harbor on the 28th of September at 1000 hours. Summers and his crew were given high praises for their unprecedented rescue, unique in submarine history, and

At Saipan the former POWs were guided up onto the deck to be transfered ashore. A few were too weak to walk and had to be carried. The clothing was donated by the crew. San Francisco Maritime National Park Association.

for a successful war patrol which earned the combat insignia. The combined total tonnage sunk of the two wolf packs was the highest to date in the war.

    Pampanito was credited with sinking three ships. Summers was awarded the Navy Cross, as were skippers Loughlin, Fluckey, Reich, and Swineburn. Fluckey went on to become the most highly decorated submariner of the war. The Navy and Marine Corps Medal was awarded

to those who swam out during the rescue, as well as to pharmacist mate Demers. The three men involved in the repair at sea of the leaky trim tank received Letters of Commendation.

Transferred to an LST for the trip ashore, the survivors' smiles and "thumbs up" were more than enough reward for Pampanito's *crew. San Francisco Maritime National Park Association.*

7

THE FOURTH
WAR PATROL
28 October - 30 December 1944

*P*ampanito went through her usual repair and reprovisioning period at Pearl Harbor. During this time the VHF radio equipment that caused problems with wolf pack communications on the previous patrol was replaced. Part of the difficulty was that the sub's radio was built to Army standards, while those of her counterparts were built to Navy standards. A new model SJ radar reflector was added.

Paul Summers, *Pampanito's* commanding officer for her first three war patrols, went home on emergency leave. After ten consecutive runs into the hazardous western Pacific, three on *Pampanito* and seven on USS *Stingray* (SS-186), he needed the time off. The responsibilities of commanding a fleet submarine and protecting the lives of its crew were demanding. Capt. Frank Wesley (Mike) Fenno, Jr. volunteered to relieve Summers.

Captain Fenno was an experienced submarine officer with an enviable war record. He was commanding officer of USS *Trout* (SS-202)

on patrol off Midway Island on December 7, 1941 when he received a radio report of the Japanese attack on Pearl Harbor. Hearing distant bombardment on Midway he thought it, too, was a target of the Japanese invasion force. In reality, it was two Japanese destroyers that heavily shelled Midway as a diversion. Unfortunately they left the scene before Captain Fenno could counterattack. In February 1942 *Trout* was ordered to Corregidor, the island fortress at the entrance to Manila Bay in the Philippines, to deliver 3,500 rounds of much needed anti-aircraft ammunition in addition to canned food, grapefruit and cigarettes.

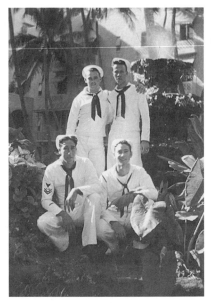

Standing, left to right, Leroy Van Housen, Bob Evans, kneeling, left to right, George Strother, Manuel Mendez, in dress whites, outside the Royal Hawaiian. Michael Manning.

Capt. Frank Wesley Fenno relieved Paul Summers as commanding officer of Pampanito *on her fourth war patrol. San Francisco Maritime National Park Association.*

There, *Trout* drew ten torpedoes and took on a very unusual ballast — more than twenty tons of gold and silver taken from Manila banks and moved to Corregidor for safekeeping. Five hundred eighty-three gold bars and heavy canvas bags containing eighteen tons of silver coins were carefully placed in *Trout*'s bilges to be delivered to Pearl Harbor. En route, *Trout* tracked and sank an enemy freighter despite rough weather and high seas. Later the same day *Trout* avoided a surprise torpedo

Trout *drew ten torpedoes and took on a very unusual ballast — more than twenty tons of gold and silver.*

attack from a Japanese patrol vessel and quickly sank the attacker. Fenno was awarded an Army Distinguished Service Cross, a Navy Cross and a Gold Star in place of a second Navy Cross. Fenno left *Trout* after four patrols and went on to command USS *Runner* (SS-275). He received an additional Gold Star for his work on *Runner*.

The *Pampanito* crew spent October 17 to 25 training with their new commanding officer. Loading of ammunition and provisions was complete by October 27 and on the afternoon of October 28 the submarine was again ready for sea. That evening *Pampanito* led a wolf pack of four U.S. submarines from Pearl Harbor, bound for the Japanese convoy routes between Hainan Island and Hong Kong, basically the same area as her previous war patrol. The wolf pack, nick-named "Fennomints" after pack commander Fenno in *Pampanito,* consisted of USS *Sea Cat* (SS-399), USS *Pipefish* (SS-388), and USS *Searaven* (SS-196). *Sea Cat,* under the command of R.R. McGreggor, was a brand new submarine on her first war patrol. *Searaven,* commanded by Lt. Commander Raymond Berthrong, was an older boat on her thirteenth run. *Pipefish,* skippered by Lt. Commander William Deragon, was making her third foray. All four were "Portsmouth boats," products of the Portsmouth Naval Shipyard.

The pack of steel sharks stopped briefly at Midway to refuel before leaving at four engine speed for Saipan. A change of orders was received on November 3, and they cut back to two engine speed, about 14½ knots. *Pipefish,* however, with an emergency case of appendicitis aboard, was released and headed full speed for Saipan.

On November 6, 1944 *Pampanito* celebrated her first anniversary at sea.

While underway, the remainder of the wolf pack was joined by *Archerfish* (SS-311) which stayed with them until they reached Saipan. She then went north to her assigned patrol zone off Honshu. Meanwhile, the Fennomints completed minor repairs and refueling at Saipan before leaving for the Bashi Channel patrol area.

Arriving north of the Philippines on November 17, the submarines set up parallel patrol lanes with *Searaven* to the west of *Pampanito* and *Pipefish* and *Sea Cat* to the east. As Japanese planes were seldom seen in this area so late in the war, the boats patrolled on the surface using a zigzagging course, constant SJ radar search, and high

Refueling at Midway and, later in the war, Saipan, allowed American submarines to stay on patrol for longer periods of time than at the beginning of the war.

periscope observations every fifteen minutes. As the pack worked its way toward the extreme western edge of the patrol area Fenno knew enemy planes were more common so he switched to a submerged routine during daylight hours.

At this stage of the war "Convoy College" was thick with American submarines. In addition to deliberately concentrating boats in the area because it was known to produce many targets, the U.S. Navy had more new submarines in service available to be sent there. During the short period of a few days, *Pampanito* exchanged signals with *Pintado* and *Halibut*, and monitored the movements of *Jallao, Atule, Haddock* and *Tuna.*

Woodrow Weaver, torpedoman 1/c: "It seemed we sighted a friendly sub every few days."

With so many American submarines operating in the area Japanese supply lines were being methodically destroyed. By the end of the war, American submarines would account for 1,300 Japanese ships — more than 5¼ million tons.

On the night of November 18, *Pipefish* reported a contact. The submarines converged on a three ship convoy; a cargo ship with an escort ahead and a smaller ship astern. *Pampanito* tracked the ships for an hour-and-a-half waiting for *Pipefish* to fire her torpedoes. *Searaven* took up a position about three miles off *Pampanito's* port quarter, also tracking the targets. *Pipefish* sent out a message that she was breaking off the attack because she picked up SJ radar interference and suspected that an enemy submarine was in the area. Fenno, more aggressive and with greater confidence in his radar equipment, sent out the message "Am attacking" and moved in from the convoy's port side.

Pampanito fired a six-torpedo spread from the bow tubes with the running depth set alternately for six and eight feet because of high seas. Fenno then swung the boat around and the stern tubes were brought to bear. While firing the four stern tubes, two hits were seen on the cargo ship, one amidships and one astern. Lookouts reported a bright orange flash followed instantly by an enormous pillar of black smoke rising more than 500 feet in the air. The fire was short-lived and in two minutes it vanished as the target disappeared from the radar. The freighter, later identified as the 1,200-ton *Shinko Maru*, sank quickly by the stern.

By the end of the war, American submarines would account for 1,300 Japanese ships — more than 5¼ million tons.

The Shinko Maru *was launched in 1935 by the Yokohama Dock Co. Propelled by a two-cycle, six cylinder diesel engine, she was rated at 4,700 horsepower. San Francisco Maritime National Park Association.*

Another hit was heard on the second target (*Banshu Maru No. 17*), but it remained afloat and moved out of visual range. Both remaining vessels were seen on radar heading at top speed toward nearby Hainan Island. *Pampanito* pulled back from the chase to reload the torpedo tubes and *Searaven* was ordered in to finish them off. During the next two hours *Searaven* attacked twice without success. The ships reached the safety of the Hainan coast.

Woodrow Weaver: "The strategy of attacking on the surface at night paid off in being able to avoid depth charges, but there was the danger of being hit by gunfire. An attack at night seemed to throw the Japanese escort ships into confusion, especially when torpedoes began to explode. The resultant confusion made it easier for the submarines."

Resuming her patrol, *Pampanito* later picked up a well-escorted convoy on the morning of November 30. The Japanese ships were tracked for more than two days without being able to set up a firing position. They were too fast and zigzagged widely. The convoy consisted of four ships in a column plus a destroyer in the lead with two smaller escorts to port and starboard of the column. All the escorts were equipped with sonar. *Pampanito's* sound operator said he heard at least five escort vessels pinging as the ships went past. To further complicate matters, the sea was flat calm and the moon was full.

Just before dawn, Fenno finally got *Pampanito* into position and fired the bow tubes at the two leading ships in the column. Swinging around, he tried to bring the stern tubes to bear on the destroyer, but the

remaining ships moved out of range before another attack could be set up. When *Pampanito* surfaced after reloading the forward torpedo tubes the rest of the Fennomints could not be located. The convoy's speed had put *Pampanito* well ahead of her pack. *Pampanito* returned to the original patrol lane and located *Searaven* later that night.

Over the next two days the weather turned from flat calm to a force 7 sea with strong northerly winds and mountainous waves. No matter how deep she went, the boat couldn't escape the effects of the weather and the constant pitching and severe rolling.

Ona Hawkins, electrician's mate 3/c: "We were in a typhoon in the South China Sea. A gallon of catsup was thrown off the counter and onto the bulkhead. It looked like we had a massacre in the crew's mess."

Two hours before dawn on December 3, *Searaven* sent out a contact report of a convoy sighted and the pack again converged. *Searaven* attacked first and reported one vessel sunk with two hits. Next, *Sea Cat* reported she sank another ship and *Searaven* commenced her second assault. *Pipefish* also reported she was attacking and *Pampanito,* moving in last, took up a position well ahead of the targets.

Pampanito's lookouts reported two bright explosions ahead over the horizon four minutes apart in the direction of *Searaven's* attack. Another explosion was heard in the direction of *Pipefish* as she sank *Coast Defense Vessel No. 64*. *Pampanito* went to battle stations at dawn as three of the ships and two escorts moved into range. Extra care was needed not to broach in the thirty-foot seas as a four-torpedo spread was fired from the after tubes at the two leading ships. A second attack was aborted as an escort charged in, driving *Pampanito* deep. A string of six depth charges exploded, none of them close.

Ona Hawkins, electrician's mate 3/c, was undergoing his first depth charging: "At first I wasn't scared, but after the first one the period between charges was agonizing — waiting to see if the next one was closer."

Woodrow Weaver, on the other hand, had been through it before: "Some depth charges were dropped, but none were close enough for concern."

Surfacing two hours later, *Pampanito* and the rest of the wolf pack searched for the remaining ships in the convoy. Later that night *Sea*

"We were in a typhoon in the South China Sea. A gallon of catsup was thrown off the counter and onto the bulkhead. It looked like we had a massacre in the crew's mess."
                                                          Ona Hawkins

Cat sank a ship damaged earlier by *Searaven.* After comparing reports, it was believed that five ships in the convoy were sunk.

The next day was spent searching for the remaining ships, but the seas were empty of everything except large waves. *Searaven,* being out of torpedoes, was released and departed for Midway. The three remaining boats resumed the patrol as the rugged seas continued.

Woodrow Weaver: "The last couple of weeks of the patrol were conducted in very heavy weather. We were operating in mountainous seas. The personnel who stood watches on the bridge would come below soaked to the skin.

"My watch station was in the forward torpedo room, so I luckily escaped the weather. On most patrols, I never saw the topside from the time we got underway until we returned to port."

During this time *Pampanito* was constantly battered by wind and waves. On the surface, the boat rolled as much as thirty degrees. The conning tower hatch was continually manned so it could be closed when seas washed over the boat. The bilge pumps ran twenty-four hours a day, and frequently it was too rough to serve anything at meals other than sandwiches. Even two hundred feet below the surface, where it was normally calm and still, the boat rolled as much as ten degrees.

Woodrow Weaver: "The heavy weather made it difficult to conduct offensive operations and a couple of opportunities were lost because of weather."

On December 10, a mine was sighted and *Pampanito* tried to sink it with her 20mm gun, but the attempt was unsuccessful. Lookouts spotted several other mines over the next few days, reporting their positions to the rest of the pack.

On December 14 it was discovered that *Pampanito* was leaving an oil slick astern. A work party investigated and found a broken pipe connecting two of the vents on No. 4 FBT fuel tank. They worked to convert the fuel tank into a main ballast tank, but the high seas made this a difficult job. In the process one man, Chief Motor Machinist's Mate William Merryman, was washed overboard, but was quickly recovered. The conversion was completed.

On December 17, *Pipefish* located a large solitary freighter and the pack gave pursuit until it slipped into the safety of a sheltered bay at Yulin, on the Hainan coast.

Now, *Pampanito* was low on fuel and, because of the beating she took in the rough weather, in need of a refit. McGreggor, in *Sea Cat* assumed command of the pack. On December 18, to the delight of the crew, *Pampanito* was ordered to Fremantle, Australia. It would be a long haul where every drop of fuel was precious, but the crew welcomed the prospect.

Their route took them from the South China Sea, through the Sulu Sea and into the Celebes Sea. On December 23, *Pampanito* passed through the Makassar Strait (between Borneo and Sulawesi) and crossed the equator for the first time. Crossing the equator called for the time-honored tradition of a visit by King Neptune and the conversion of the crew's pollywogs into shellbacks. Pollywogs, those who have never crossed the equator, were called before the court of King Neptune and initiated into the "mysteries of the deep" by the shellbacks, those who had crossed before. The court accused the novices of various transgressions: "being a non-coffee-making mess cook," "spreading pollywog tracks all over the bridge," and so on. Of course, they were found guilty and

The code machine had to be destroyed before going through Lombok Strait. San Francisco Maritime National Park Association.

punished accordingly. Punishment included drinking a concoction brewed for the occasion from hot sauce and other condiments, crawling on their hands and knees through a gauntlet of paddles while wearing only skivvies and sitting in a wired "hot seat." It was a good-humored way to relieve tension and enjoyed by all.

Elmer Smith, torpedoman 2/c: "The initiations were funny. Especially swallowing the oyster on a string that had been soaked in hot sauce."

Because the waters they traveled through were shallow and the surrounding islands mostly

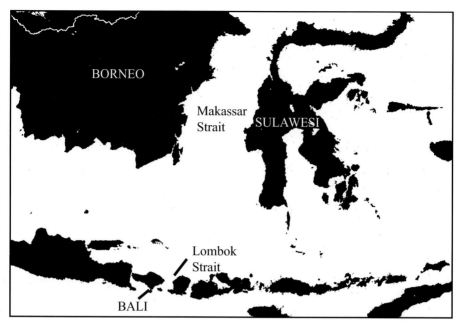

Ordered to Fremantle, Australia at the end of her fourth war patrol, Pampanito *crossed the equator east of Borneo, through the Makassar Strait. Continuing south, the crew destroyed her code machine and code books before going through the treacherous Japanese-held Lombok Strait.*

occupied by the Japanese, it was standard practice to destroy the ship's code machine, code books and ciphers when forced to traverse them. Radioman Mervin Hill broke the machine into pieces and threw them over the side. The other materials were burned.

Roger Walters, radioman 3/c: "All of our communications, secret code communications and everything had to be destroyed in order for us to go down to Lombok Straits. We were controlling one side of the straits but the Japanese had the other side. It was a fairly narrow channel. So we had to destroy all of our communications equipment so in the event we were captured by the Japanese they wouldn't have our top secret information. Lt. Red was communications officer at the time. He had me go back to the after torpedo room with all these papers that had to be burned. We're back there, we've got a big basket, an incinerator basket and we're burning papers and of course we end up with a lot of ashes. So we've got to take these ashes and flush 'em over the side. There's a head in the after torpedo room. So I said, 'Mr. Red, I'll flush the ashes out.'

"'No, that's all, Walters. I know how to do this.'

"He takes these ashes and he starts dumping them in the head. There's a flapper valve in there, you have to pull the handle down, drop the stuff in, flush it down, bring the flapper valve up, open the outer sea valve, build up some pressure and then pull the handle and flush the stuff out to sea. This is all great except that he didn't clear the chamber before he pulled the handle and the valve wasn't seated. He's got brand clean khakis on, oh, just clean, all spiffed up. He has to lean over this thing in order to pull it. He leaned right into it and he pulled the handle and, wham! it all comes right back up and he was just ashes from head to foot."

Pampanito moved on into the Indian Ocean through the Lombok Strait east of Bali. The strait was eleven miles wide and twenty-seven miles long. Minefields on either side constricted the passage to a much narrower area.

Harry Bowring, motor machinist's mate 2/c: "This Strait had to be negotiated in one night, because you had to be just above the water and visible to be able to navigate this in one night's time. Submerged would take you too long to get through because of the slower speed when submerged. The Japanese could easily shoot you out of the water if they got sight of you."

Ona Hawkins, electrician's mate 3/c: "That was a frightening experience."

Christmas Day found them safely in the Indian Ocean. Two days later they approached a fuel barge at Exmouth Gulf. Located at the northwestern-most tip of Australia, Exmouth Gulf was conceived as an advance submarine base earlier in the war. During the winter

As can be seen, a submarine toilet is a complicated device, involving piping, valves and a knowledge of just how they work. San Francisco Maritime National Park Association.

In front of the Ocean Beach Hotel, Cottesloe, Perth, West Australia. Standing, left to right, Ona Hawkins, James Behney, Harold Chinn, Manuel Mendez; kneeling, left to right, Edmund Stockslader, Albert Bacskay. Michael Manning.

monsoon it was subjected to northwesterlies that made submarine docking difficult. Nevertheless, in 1943 it was built up with landing strips, quarters, a first-aid station, radio, power plant, water distillers, anti-aircraft installations and a fuel barge. In May of that year, the sub-tender USS *Pelias* (AS14) arrived from Fremantle. But as soon as the Japanese found out about the operation they made it the target of their long-range bombers which quickly put an end to the concept. When *Pampanito* arrived, running the last few miles on fumes and batteries, only the radio shack and fuel barge remained.

After taking on enough fuel to reach Fremantle, *Pampanito* sailed December 28. As she neared the Australian port two days later the crew was met by a small provision ship that transferred morale-boosting supplies: Australian beer, milk, fresh fruits and vegetables.

Woodrow Weaver: "There were a number of U.S. submarines operating out of Fremantle, and COMSUBPAC had contracted for a couple of hotels to be used by the recuperating submarine sailors at the end of a patrol. We went to the Ocean Beach Hotel near Fremantle, and spent two very pleasant weeks."

Much to the crew's surprise they were joyously greeted by a cheering group of the former POWs rescued by *Pampanito* on her third patrol.

Woodrow Weaver: "Perth is within a few miles of Fremantle and we were able to contact some of the Aussie war prisoners who lived in the area. They threw quite a celebration for us."

Clarence A. Smith: "To put in to Fremantle on the next patrol and meet about twenty or twenty-five of them down there. The word was

Much to the crew's surprise they were joyously greeted by a cheering group of the former POWs rescued by Pampanito *on her third patrol.*

there before we got there. I didn't get out with any of them but any number of the crew did. And seeing how they had filled out and had a few good meals in them …"

William Fisk, engineman 2/c: "After the POWs got back to Australia, we were the talk of the country. When we came in, everyone that was in the vicinity visited. It was a pleasant experience. There was one fella, came down, had his wife and baby with him. He had a young son. It was great to see something that turned out good. That was my most satisfying war patrol. I enjoyed seeing those guys saved more than I did sinking a ship."

This liberty is one that *Pampanito*'s crew still talks about today.

Pampanito's fourth patrol was a success and officers and crew were congratulated, with Captain Fenno being awarded the Bronze Star. The patrol was a long one both in terms of time and miles; she was out sixty-three days and covered 16,406 miles.

"After the POWs got back to Australia, we were the talk of the country. When we came in, everyone that was in the vicinity visited. It was great to see something that turned out good."
William Fisk

8

THE FIFTH WAR PATROL
23 January - 12 February 1945

Paul Summers returned to command *Pampanito* on January 2, 1945. Lt. Landon L. Davis, executive officer (XO) on the first four patrols, was relieved by Lt. Cdr. Lynn Orser. Lt. Cdr. William Bush reported aboard as prospective commanding officer (PCO).

Pampanito was refitted, repaired, refueled and reloaded. The torpedoes were a disappointment. Woodrow Weaver, torpedoman 1/c: "Our torpedo load consisted of sixteen Mark 14 steam torpedoes in the forward torpedo room and eight Mark 18 electric torpedoes in the after room. Our CO would have preferred a full load of electric torpedoes, but they were not available in sufficient quantity in Fremantle."

Fuel and torpedoes were taken aboard without difficulty. The food was a different matter. Woodrow Weaver: "As we were loading torpedoes and supplies for the fifth patrol, a fire broke out on the pier about fifty yards from us. West Australia is very dry and the wooden pier was in flames within a few minutes. We had just completed loading our

Paul E. Summers in uniform of full commander, taken about the time he returned for Pampanito's *fifth patrol. San Francisco Maritime National Park Association.*

torpedoes but most of the food supplies were still on deck. We had to get underway to clear the dock. The supplies were hurriedly struck below as we moved out into the bay. After a couple of hours, we were allowed to come back alongside the pier as the fire seemed to be under control. The cooks had their working party bring everything topside again so they could rearrange things in some semblance of order. As soon as they were ready to start taking things below, the fire broke out again. We had to get underway and it was a rush to get the decks clear once more. The poor cooks gave up after that and left things as they were. They had considerable trouble locating specific food items during the fifth patrol."

Included in the repairs was replacement of the after 20mm antiaircraft gun by a single-barrel 40mm gun. By January 14 the boat was ready for sea and the next week was spent in training and gunnery exercises.

USS Guavina *(SS-362) as she appeared in 1955 while refueling a P5M Patrol Seaplane in the open sea. U.S. Navy.*

The fifth war patrol carried Pampanito *through Lombok and Karimata Straits and into the Gulf of Siam.*

Departing Fremantle on January 23, *Pampanito* was accompanied by USS *Guavina* (SS-362), under the command of Cdr. Ralph H. Lockwood. Training continued as the two submarines practiced night approaches with the Australian minesweeper HMAS *Warnambool*. The minesweeper left after the first day and the two boats made for Exmouth Bay to top off their diesel fuel. Arriving January 26, they spent ten hours refueling, then *Pampanito* and *Guavina* motored north toward the Lombok and Karimata Straits.

Summers had a dry sense of humor. Well rested after having a patrol off, it came out more frequently than on earlier patrols. Gordon

Hopper, newly promoted to quartermaster 3/c, recalled an incident involving painting camouflage on the periscope shears. "I was sent up the periscope shears with a bucket of paint and brush to re-camouflage the scope heads. When a larger than usual swell hit us and rolled the boat I grabbed for support and dropped the can of paint that landed on the deck, inches from Captain Summers who was watching the whole thing. He was spattered with marine blue from head to foot. He screamed, 'Hopper, why did you do that?'

"I responded, 'Captain, it was the paint or me.'

"'Better it had been you,' he growled and then shouted down the conning tower hatch, 'Send up a .45.'

"'Aye, aye, captain.'

"'Belay that,' Summers said. 'If I had a .45 there'd be a dead quartermaster up here.'

"It wasn't funny [to me] at the time but hilarious in retrospect. And, of course, from that incident on I was first in line for every dirty detail."

Lombok Strait was quickly negotiated on the evening of January 29, taking only two and a half hours from one end to the other. Karimata Strait, between Borneo and Belitung Island was cleared two nights later. On the morning of February 1, signals were exchanged with USS *Bluegill* (SS-242) and USS *Bream* (SS-243).

That afternoon they again crossed the equator and the new pollywogs that came aboard in Fremantle were initiated. Summers played the role of King Neptune in a ceremony held in the crew's mess. The pollywogs were given the usual treatment of foul-tasting potions, partially-shaved heads, electric hot seats and other shenanigans designed to welcome them into the realm of King Neptune and make them shellbacks.

Continuing northward, *Guavina* and *Pampanito* filled each day with training and practice approaches. The new camouflage paint was found to be surprisingly effective.

On February 3, as they reached their assigned patrol area in the Gulf of Siam off the coast of the Malay Peninsula, a mine was sighted. The crew fired on it with both 40mms, but it would not sink despite several direct hits. Later that day, several dozen bales of raw rubber were

The galley has just about enough space to turn around in. Above, crockery storage on the left with spices in the background, right, ovens, stove, deep fryer and scale. Author.

sighted and Summers noted in the patrol report that he was tempted to pick up this precious material.

Food was excellent on *Pampanito*, as it was on all American submarines. The "open ice box" policy let the crew have anything they wanted at any time of the day.

Harry Bowring, motor machinist's mate 2/c: "We were fed well due to the lack of natural sunlight. Food was very good. Coffee and soup were always available, twenty-four hours a day."

Manuel Mendez, torpedoman 3/c: "The food was the very best that our nation could offer."

Earl Watkins, motor machinist's mate 2/c: "It was the very best. We had a baker on board so we had fresh bread and rolls every day."

Woodrow Weaver: "The food was excellent. Great care was taken to see that submarines were well supplied with the best of food."

In addition, the cooks were well-trained and highly qualified. In an extremely confined area, they produced three meals a day for a crew of seventy to eighty men.

Gordon Hopper, quartermaster 3/c: "Cooks and bakers were outstanding and subs were allotted extra good rations."

"The food was the very best that our nation could offer."
Manuel Mendez
"We had fresh bread and rolls every day."
Earl Watkins

Unfortunately, food quality was limited by the lack of refrigerated storage space on a submarine. Typically, fresh produce and milk ran out far too soon.

Radio technician 2/c Spencer Stimler: "We had fresh food after we started on patrol. But it didn't last too long."

Elmer Smith, torpedoman 2/c: "On long patrols we usually ran out."

Manuel Mendez, torpedoman 3/c: "Sometimes it did not last as long as the war patrols and it was then that we missed it most of all.

Part of the "best available" provisioning in Fremantle included Australian mutton, something foreign to American tastes. Spencer Stimler remembered it this way: "We were

Across a passageway from the galley are some of the lockers, refrigerated and dry, for food storage. Every square inch of space is utilized. Author.

told it was lamb. I've eaten bear meat that smelled better and certainly tasted better. The cooks tried their best, but when the meat was put on your plate the fat congealed and eating lard would have been a treat. Plus there was the additional problem of getting the meat past your nose. It was really, really bad."

On the night of February 6, a column of smoke was sighted which proved to be from Japanese convoy HI 88D consisting of *Engen Maru, Taigyo Maru, Haruyasa Maru* and their escorts: the Mikura-Class *Yashiro,* and the Type-C *No. 13* and *No. 31.* A multi-stacked ship was smoking heavily through one funnel, which was helpful in tracking the convoy of three ships and four escorts. It was too dark for a periscope attack, so Summers risked moving in as close as possible on the surface. It was a dangerous situation as the water was quite shallow. Woodrow Weaver: "The water depth was only about thirty fathoms (180 feet) and our skipper was reluctant to make a submerged approach as he did not have sufficient depth of water to go deep if we were detected. The

"We were told it was lamb. I've eaten bear meat that smelled better and certainly tasted better."

Spencer Stimler

conditions dictated a surface attack at night; however, the conditions for a surface attack were not to our advantage. The seas were very calm and there was a full moon. It made it difficult to get within close firing range. Torpedoes in the forward tubes were ordered set on low speed, which increased their range, and were fired at the target from about 5,000 yards."

Once in position, *Pampanito* fired at the leading ship, the 6,968-ton tanker *Engen Maru,* and scored two hits. She sank in minutes taking with her 7,110 tons of crude oil, 1,195 tons of rubber and 217 tons of copper. The escorts exchanged light signals and the convoy changed course, steaming out of radar range.

Woodrow Weaver: "We reloaded the forward tubes and continued in pursuit of the convoy."

As Summers set up another attack, two of the escorts moved in quickly on the port beam. *Pampanito's* bow tubes were fired at the two leading ships and she pulled clear of the escorts, which apparently were not equipped with radar as they had trouble locating *Pampanito*. No hits were heard. The crew's frustration increased when the last four torpedoes forward were fired at the convoy, but again there were no hits.

Woodrow Weaver: "We fired the remaining torpedoes in the forward room. Since we were firing from extreme range, coupled with the fact the convoy escorts had been alerted by the first attack, the target ships could see the approaching torpedoes and turned to avoid them. The result was no further hits from our remaining ten torpedoes. A submarine skipper hated to waste that many torpedoes, and ours was pretty unhappy. He could not use the electric torpedoes in the after room without closing the range considerably. The electric torpedo range was about 3,500 yards. As a result, the two remaining ships made their escape."

Pampanito pulled away and *Guavina* moved in. From *Pampanito's* bridge two hits were seen on the larger of the two remaining ships, the 6900-ton freighter *Taigyo Maru,* and it disappeared from the radar screen.

With the forward torpedo room empty and the after one full, Summers thought it might be worthwhile to transfer some of the after torpedoes to the forward room. They were too large and heavy to be pulled the length of the boat internally. The only way the transfer could

This artist's rendering of the sinking of the Engen Maru *captures the essence of a surface night attack. San Francisco Maritime National Park Association.*

be accomplished was to take the torpedoes out of the after torpedo loading hatch and put them in the forward torpedo loading hatch. This involved rigging the torpedo loading boom over the after hatch, removing a torpedo, setting it in the sub's rubber boat, floating it forward, moving the boom forward, taking the torpedo out of the boat and lowering it into the forward torpedo room. As the captain wanted four torpedoes moved, this meant going through the process four times, in the hostile waters of the Gulf of Siam.

Woodrow Weaver: "It was a hare-brained scheme, and our torpedo officer tried to talk Commander Summers out of it, to no avail. I had a personal stake in this also. I had been told I would be advanced to chief petty officer at the end of the fifth patrol. I could very well see, as I would be very much involved in this torpedo transfer, my chances of making chief going down the drain should the operation prove to be disastrous. The chances of it happening were very good. All we had to

do was lose control of one of those torpedoes, in trying to balance it on the rubber boat, and it would be gone. Each torpedo weighed 3,000 pounds. I was worried that the rubber boat could not float them without sinking."

As dawn approached on February 7, *Pampanito* dove and continued the patrol routine while the torpedo transfer was studied, then scheduled.

Woodrow Weaver: "The skipper was determined to make the attempt to transfer the torpedoes. On the night of the 7th of February, we assembled our torpedo transfer working party in the forward torpedo room."

When *Pampanito* surfaced at dusk a message from *Guavina* was received that the smoke of a possible convoy had been sighted.

Woodrow Weaver: "As we prepared to go topside, the radar operator in the conning tower reported a ship contact. The CO rushed to the bridge, and we were spared the torpedo transfer operation by the skin of our teeth."

Summers set a new course to intercept. A little later a high periscope observation revealed the northbound convoy on the horizon: one medium cargo ship and two escorts. When *Pampanito* arrived, distant flashes were seen as one of the escorts fired at *Guavina* following her first unsuccessful attack.

Woodrow Weaver: "The ship contact proved to be a single oil tanker with two escorts. The same conditions of a calm sea and bright moonlight prevailed. We made an approach as close as we could."

Summers moved in and fired four electric torpedoes from the stern tubes, but no hits were heard.

Woodrow Weaver: "The range was at least 3,000 yards and we missed again. Our skipper was fit to be tied. Luckily the escorts had not been alerted, as the electric torpedoes left no telltale wake."

Just before midnight Summers sent a message to *Guavina* and requested that she fire a signal from the very pistol to draw off the starboard escort. *Guavina* complied with enthusiasm, firing four flares from her "Buck Rogers" [flare or very pistol] gun. The escort went to investigate the flares, the target zigged to port and *Pampanito* attacked. She was in position just after midnight. From the patrol report:

0025 Fired three torpedoes aft from 4000 yards on 75 starboard track.

0029 Had just about checked off three misses when the first torpedo hit and simultaneously the ship disintegrated with the bow going one way and stern in the opposite direction and most of the ship going straight up. Judging from the intense flames and explosions, this ship was evidently loaded with aviation gasoline. One escort was close enough, I'm sure, to share in the effects of the explosions. The second torpedo probably hit whatever was left to hit. The whole area looked like a fourth of July celebration and we felt slightly naked in all this gaslight. Escort on starboard quarter commenced firing at us and placed several rounds just over the bridge before we could pull clear on all four main engines. For the next twenty minutes one violent explosion followed another as the ship was torn to pieces. The stern sank and the bow put on the finishing touch by exploding beautifully and in Technicolor.

Pampanito had sunk the *Eifuku Maru*, a 3,520-ton gunboat.

The remaining escort located *Pampanito*. Because of shallow water Summers didn't want to dive. The only option was to outrun the escort on the surface. He called down for maximum speed and began trying to outdistance the escort's salvoes. Knowing the enemy would compensate for its misses, Summers steered the boat toward each splash. In that way each new salvo was aimed at where the submarine was previously, while the submarine maneuvered in the direction of the earlier salvo.

Woodrow Weaver: "We had a slight speed advantage and managed to outrun the escort. He was firing his deck gun and several shells sailed over us. Again we were lucky that his gunnery was not too good. We escaped after a forty-five minute chase."

With only one torpedo remaining, the storage skids were empty. *Author.*

"The whole area looked like a fourth of July celebration and we felt slightly naked in all this gaslight."

Paul Summers, War Patrol Log

Some of the crew gathered for a photo the day after arriving at Subic Bay, Philippine Islands. Standing, left to right, unidentified, John Madaras, unidentified, unidentified, Manuel Mendez, William Fisk, Joseph Higgins, Clarence Carmody, unidentified, George Moffett. Seated, left to right, unidentified, unidentified, Albert Bacskay, Paul Pappas, unidentified, unidentified, unidentified. Michael Manning.

With only one torpedo remaining for emergencies, *Pampanito* was ordered to proceed to the southeast corner of the patrol area to await further instructions. Although initially scheduled for a return to Fremantle, on February 11, orders were received to proceed to Subic Bay, Philippines for refit.

Subic Bay had recently been recaptured and plans were being developed to establish a submarine base there. An advance contingent arrived on February 11th and *Pampanito* arrived on the afternoon of the 12th and tied up alongside the submarine tender USS *Griffin* (AS-13) becoming the first submarine to refit in Subic Bay.

Woodrow Weaver: "Our stay alongside the *Griffin* was short also. We were in Subic about two weeks. We did not turn the boat over to a relief crew, but did our own work in preparation for the sixth patrol. We did take time for a trip to the beach for a picnic. It was a secure area free of Japanese control. There were Japanese troops in the general area, and MacArthur's forces were fighting for Manila."

Again, officers and crew were congratulated for a successful patrol. *Pampanito* was credited with two ships sunk. The fifth patrol was short, only 20 days, but *Pampanito* had traveled almost 6,500 miles since leaving Australia.

9

THE SIXTH WAR PATROL
25 February - 24 April 1945

While *Pampanito* prepared for her next patrol, the last Japanese destroyer sunk by submarines during the war, *Nokaze,* was torpedoed on February 20 by *Pargo*, near Cam Ranh Bay, Indo-China (now Vietnam). Japan started the war with 113 destroyers and built new ones during the hostilities, but now had only thirty-seven remaining. Thirty-nine destroyers were victims of submarines.

Pampanito departed for her sixth patrol on the afternoon of February 25, 1945 and returned to her previous hunting grounds, off the Malay Peninsula. On February 27, following orders received the day before, Cdr. Summers sent a message to *Sealion* (SS-315), and *Mingo* (SS-216) to rendezvous. They met three days later and Summers, commander of the new wolf pack, gave orders for their patrol of the area. The boats traveled in parallel lanes with Lt. Cdr. Charles F. Putman in *Sealion* to the west, and Lt. Cdr. John R. Madison in *Mingo* to the east.

This unusual overhead photo of Pintado *(SS-387) shows the boat underway on the surface on a bright day. Undated, it was probably taken during sea trials in late 1943.* Pampanito, *being of the same class, would have cut a similar swath on the surface. National Archives.*

After several days, their only sighting was a properly marked hospital ship, which they let pass, and a group of six sailing ships, which they avoided. Then they met two U.S. subs, *Pintado* (SS-387) and *Sea Robin* (SS-407). *Pampanito* rendezvoused with *Sea Robin* on March 11, receiving forty-six sacks of long overdue mail. The mail was originally sent to Saipan but *Pampanito* was in Fremantle when it arrived. The mail

was then forwarded to Fremantle only to arrive there as the sub entered Subic Bay. But now, Christmas finally caught up with *Pampanito*. The crew was delighted and morale soared, even though some of the Christmas cakes and cookies were a bit moldy.

Woodrow Weaver, torpedoman 1/c: "The mail had been sent to Fremantle, but we missed it when we were ordered into Subic Bay. We transferred forty-six bags of mail. When you consider our crew numbered eighty, it worked out to about half a bag of mail per man.

"I remember getting some fried chicken from my sister, Josephine, which she had mailed in October 1944. She had the foresight to seal it in cans and it arrived in good condition. Many of the crew received fruitcakes. Most of the sailors were not familiar with the keeping quality of fruit cakes, and they threw them into the trash cans to be dumped overboard. I sent my forward torpedo room crew back to the crew's mess with instructions to salvage as much fruit cake as they could. We soon had a two foot high mound of fruit cake which we enjoyed the remainder of the patrol."

With little action, life aboard settled into a simple routine of watch-standing and filling the hours off watch. Most of the crew played card games, read, wrote letters, re-read the Christmas letters and talked.

Robert Bennett, torpedoman 1/c: "There was good fellowship with your shipmates and a sense of pride."

Gordon Hopper, quartermaster 1/c: "There were days of boredom, listening and looking for Japanese shipping, punctuated by brief periods of intensive activity — the attack, the depth charging, evasive tactics. Lots of reading, conversation, games, sleeping."

Earl Watkins, motor machinist's mate 2/c: "To say the least, we were very close together, just like family. I never became bored. I don't remember one time that we had any conflict between the men on board. You had to like sub duty."

Others studied to advance their rating or qualify for the submariner's dolphin insignia.

Ona Hawkins, electrician's mate 3/c: "I was busy preparing for qualifications for sub dolphins and EM 3/c rate."

Occasionally there were field days, when everything had to be cleaned. And some were given extra duties to perform. Manuel Mendez,

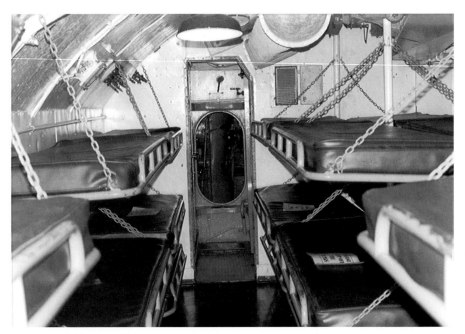

Crew berthing area where the off-duty crew slept or read mail, magazines and books. Author.

torpedoman 3/c: "Bob Evans and I upon leaving Fremantle, Australia on January 23, 1945, having been such 'cut-ups,' that although we were amongst the senior men on board we were assigned additional duties, usually given to new arrivals. Bob was assigned as a mess boy and I was given the responsibility of keeping the head just after the after battery clean. I went to the machinist's mates and asked for boiler compound that I knew they used mixed with water to keep the oil off the outer skin of the diesel engines. This cut my maintenance time by seventy-five percent, wiping everything in sight. At the end of the fifth patrol, upon arriving in port, the head was sparkling, since the compound mixture had eaten all the paint off the bulkheads and was now down to the bare metal."

Those off watch were expected to keep everything on board repaired, maintained and ready; from clearing electrical grounds to charging torpedoes to taking battery readings to mixing bread dough to cleaning bilges to checking pumps, air compressors and air conditioners to maintaining the diesel engines (if operating on batteries) or maintaining batteries (if operating on diesels).

The mess room where off-duty crew played cards, checkers and cribbage, told stories and ate. Note the pinup of Betty Grable on the bulkhead and that even the seats were storage compartments. Author.

With the Japanese Air Force and Navy depleted, it was considered safe to stay on the surface. In fact, most of this patrol was spent on the surface. Spencer Stimler, radio technician 2/c: "We were on the surface almost all the time. We would only dive to trim the boat."

But another danger lurked in the South China Sea — mines. Spencer Stimler: "Mines had broken loose and were floating. We could see them on the radar and the lookouts could spot them during the day. At night when we couldn't see, the thought of the mines floating past was enough to keep even the deepest sleepers awake."

Manuel Mendez: "Many will tell you that depth-charging is the most frightening experience, but unless you have found yourself submerged in a mine-field and hear the cable lines scraping along the hull, you haven't lived."

The next week was again one of boredom. No targets were sighted until March 18 when a contact was picked up on the SJ radar at a range of eight miles. It was traveling fast, twenty-two knots, and zigzagging wildly. Summers thought it was probably a destroyer. He tried to get closer but the target quickly disappeared over the horizon. As a result of missing the contact, Summers regrouped the pack, placing the boats in a staggered, rather than parallel configuration.

The hunting wasn't bad for everyone, *Sealion* reported she sank the unescorted tanker *Samui*, on the morning of the 17th.

Woodrow Weaver: "The *Sealion* was the only sub in the pack that was able to find anything to attack. The last few months of the war we had a lot of submarines coming up zero on their patrols. There were no targets."

"Many will tell you that depth-charging is the most frightening experience, but unless you have found yourself submerged in a mine-field and hear the cable lines scraping along the hull, you haven't lived."

Manuel Mendez

On the night of March 23, the wolf pack was joined by a fourth boat, USS *Caiman* (SS-323). *Pampanito* rendezvoused with the new member of the pack a few miles east of the small island of Pulau Redang, and Lt. Cdr. William Bush, Prospective Commanding Officer (PCO) aboard *Pampanito,* was transferred to her. Two days later control of the wolf pack was turned over to Bush in *Caiman* with *Pampanito* heading north to patrol alone until new orders were received. On March 28, *Pampanito* was ordered to Pearl Harbor by way of Saipan. En route, heavy seas and high northwest winds were encountered. On March 31, she exchanged recognition signals with USS *Snook* (SS-279). Sadly, *Snook* was lost with all hands a few days later. The storm tapered off as *Pampanito* arrived in Saipan on April 5th for fuel.

After a one day layover, the sub continued on toward Hawaii. Her return was interrupted as *Pampanito* was ordered to join a wolf pack called "Bennet's Blazers," made up of USS *Sea Owl* (SS-405), USS *Piranha* (SS-389), USS *Puffer* (SS-268), and USS *Thresher* (SS-200). The wolf pack was convened as the result of an Ultra message which indicated a Japanese submarine would make a desperate run with supplies for the enemy garrison on Wake Island. Somehow the enemy I-class boat got past the group. But *Sea Owl* spotted her unloading supplies in the island's lagoon. A well-aimed torpedo sent her to the bottom.

It was during this interlude off Wake that news of President Roosevelt's death came over the radio. Woodrow Weaver: "It was sobering news. Most of the young sailors on board had never known another president in the White House. President Truman was an unknown quantity. We were to gain a lot of respect for him, and the hard decisions he had to make a few months later."

With the sinking of the Japanese sub, the wolf pack was disbanded and *Pampanito* continued on to Pearl Harbor. To pass the time and provide a bit of recreation, some of the crew built a still to produce homemade liquor. Although against regulations, stills were fairly common on Navy ships during the war. Usually the ingredients were water, raisins, sugar and yeast, so the result was called "raisin jack."

Harry Bowring: "Drinking was not allowed on the boat but boys will be boys and one time we made illegal raisin jack. We made it from raisins that we stole from the cook — we had a really good time with this raisin jack."

Although against regulations, stills were fairly common on Navy ships during the war. Usually the ingredients were water, raisins, sugar and yeast, so the result was called "raisin jack."

After six war patrols, Pampanito *pointed her bow toward Pearl Harbor and then San Francisco. There, she would be drydocked and repaired, readied for the closing days of the war. Although this photo was taken just after the POW rescue on the third patrol (note oily hand prints on conning tower fairwater) it is representative of the boat underway on the surface, just as when she headed for Pearl Harbor. San Francisco Maritime National Park Association.*

Pampanito's still was in the engine room and it either fell over in a rough sea or was accidentally knocked over, depending on who is telling the story. In any case, a fire rapidly erupted as the alcohol ran across the floor plates and into the bilges. Fortunately, the engine men reacted quickly. They immediately sealed off the compartment and put the fire out.

George Moffett remembered it this way: "The motor macs were running off alcohol down in the after engine room. We took a certain

swell and it dumped the still. It was running into the hotplate, the damn thing caught on fire, and here we had burning alcohol all over everything. There is cork under the paint on the hull. There is a one-inch layer of cork there. Mostly insulation to keep the thing from sweating. So the motor macs all vacated the engine room, closed the doors, dogged the air conditioning. They waited for the flames to extinguish. Then they came though the boat and woke up every other motor mac in the boat, they got a paint party and they repainted the whole damn engine room. The whole inside. Happened in the middle of the night."

Although undated, this Pampanito *photo was most likely taken late in the war and somewhere near the Territory of Hawaii; both circumstances making it safer for a swim party. Even so, the American flag was flown behind the conning tower to prevent attack by friendly planes, and lookouts are posted "just in case." San Francisco Maritime National Park Association.*

Somehow the officers never learned of the incident.

Arriving at Pearl Harbor on April 24 the captain and crew were congratulated on a safe return from a hard and boring patrol.

To the crew's delight, *Pampanito* was ordered to San Francisco for a much needed Navy yard overhaul at Hunters Point. Woodrow Weaver: "The crew was elated at the prospects of being in the States again with leave time being uppermost in everyone's mind.

"Our torpedo officer informed me I was to be rated chief petty officer on our arrival in San Francisco. I was to join the "Tojo chief" ranks.[1] When we arrived in Pearl, I purchased a CPO hat and put it in my locker and looked at it every day. I could not put it on until we got to San Francisco, but I was enjoying the anticipation."

Everyone looked forward to San Francisco. The fact that they would spend only one night in Pearl Harbor with its opportunities for "rest and recreation" was considered a minor disappointment to the crew. They knew they would each have thirty days leave when they returned to the States. Anticipation was keen.

---

[1] Before the war, advancement was determined by Navy-wide examination. Those who made the highest marks were advanced to fill a quota. During the war, commanding officers were authorized to advance men without exam. Chief petty officers so promoted were called "Tojo chiefs" by white hat sailors. The thinking was that they would not have advanced but for General Tojo, Japan's wartime leader.

10

THE LAST PATROL
20 July - 1 September 1945

The entrance to San Francisco Bay was one of the most welcome sights of the war to returning service men. As many of the off duty crew as could fit crowded the narrow deck of *Pampanito* as she came under the Golden Gate Bridge. It was 0700 May 3, 1945. For some it had been a few months since they left the States but they were months that seemed like years. For those who made all six patrols it seemed a lifetime.

At Hunters Point, half the crew was given thirty days leave, the remaining half would have their turn when the first group returned. Supplies and torpedoes were unloaded as *Pampanito* was prepared for drydocking. Woodrow Weaver, in charge of unloading the torpedoes, donned his new chief's hat.

Woodrow Weaver: "The torpedoes were being lifted off by a crane. The procedure was to unload one torpedo forward then move the crane aft to take a torpedo from the after room, alternating, until all torpedoes were unloaded. I proudly wore my (*continued on page 134*)

Overhaul and drydocking at Hunter's Point Naval Shipyard in San Francisco was an opportune time for a group photo and a few individual ones, too. The above photo was taken in September, 1945, after the war. San Francisco Maritime National Park Association.

A sense of just how hectic drydocking can be is seen above, with scaffolding, wires, ducts, rope and equipment strewn everywhere. Modifications to Navy vessels are always photographed and marked as in the photo below showing Pampanito *just after drydocking. San Francisco Maritime National Park Association.*

In this Navy photo showing modifications, one gets a sense of the size of the boat looking forward from aft. San Francisco Maritime National Park Association.

(continued from page 131) new chief's hat as I moved back and forth on deck. There was a pretty stiff breeze blowing, and my brand new hat blew over the side. I was devastated. I looked pretty silly trying to fish my hat out of the water. I finished my torpedo unloading duties that day with a much bedraggled headpiece. It was embarrassing but I survived. My shipmates had a good laugh at my expense."

Once in the drydock and out of the water, the process of a major refit began. *Pampanito*'s main four-inch deck gun, which she carried forward of the conning tower on all six patrols, was replaced with a five-inch gun aft. She was fitted out with twin forty-millimeter guns, one on each gun deck, and a double twenty millimeter gun on the forward main deck. A sonar dome was installed as was a newly developed SV type radar. She was also given a load of twenty-four new acoustic torpedoes. Considered state of the art at the time, acoustic torpedoes homed on sound. They could be shot at a target and would home in on the noise of its propeller turning, without the sub's crew having to pre-select angles, depths and so on.

Paul Summers was transferred as commanding officer to the newly built USS *Cusk* (SS-348), in New London, Connecticut. He was replaced by Cdr. Donald A. Scherer, a veteran of USS *Pike* (SS-173), USS *Lapon* (SS-260) and USS *Permit* (SS-178).

Sea trials are usually done after major modifications to make sure everything operates as intended. San Francisco Maritime National Park Association.

    Pampanito left Hunters Point and headed for Pearl Harbor on July 20. Although it was common knowledge the war was nearly over, most of the crew believed they would be part of the invasion of the Japanese homeland. Their suspicions were confirmed when, on arrival at Pearl Harbor, modifications were begun for the final battle. A mine detecting sonar was mounted on the boat and deflectors were added to prevent the cables of anchored mines from being snagged in the bow and stern planes. Woodrow Weaver: "The word was we would be going into the inland sea of Japan where the waters were sowed with mines."

    The crew of *Pampanito* was preparing for training runs on August 6 when word was received of the bombing at Hiroshima. Three days later they heard about Nagasaki. They were relieved. Now, surely, the war would end even sooner.

    And on August 14 it did. Most of the crew were at the sub base outdoor movie, waiting for the feature to begin. Suddenly, the harbor was filled with the sound of ships' whistles and sirens, bellowing in the night. The sky was filled with enough multi-colored pyrotechnics from flares and rockets to equal the most

---

FM SONAR

    Frequency Modulated (FM) sonar was developed to locate mines for surface minesweepers. Because it gave bearing data on a target, much like a radar did on surface targets, scientists at the Naval Research Laboratory in San Diego modified the device for use on submarines. By May of 1945 submarines were being equipped with the device, the first use being by a nine-submarine wolf pack in Operation Barney in the Sea of Japan.

Suddenly, the harbor was filled with the sound of ships' whistles and sirens, bellowing in the night.

extravagant Fourth of July celebration. Woodrow Weaver: "Sailors in the submarine base barracks were raising cain, and the sub base commander drove up in his jeep to try to quell the noise. They picked him up and threw him in the swimming pool. He crawled out, got back in his jeep, and left them to their celebration.

"It had been a long and cruel war. There had been great loss of life, not only by those in military service, but among civilian populations also. In later years, President Truman was criticized for making the decision to drop the atom bomb on Japan. In my mind, he did the right thing. Without the effect of the atom bomb, a successful conclusion to the war would have required invading the Japanese home islands. Such an assault would have cost thousands of American lives. His decision had personal significance for me as it kept us out of those mine fields for

A great source of pride at the decommissioning party was Pampanito's *battle flag. In addition to the name of the boat and her emblem, the number 73 over a red cross indicates how many POW's were saved, the six flags on the left are the number of enemy ships she was credited with sinking in battle while those on the right are the number of ships she damaged. San Francisco Maritime National Park Association.*

which our sub was being prepared. In my estimation, President Truman's handling of the atomic bomb added greatly to his stature as a president."

Three weeks later *Pampanito* returned to San Francisco for layup and decommissioning. Officially decommissioned at Mare Island on December 15, there was a party to celebrate the occasion. It was a chance for the crew to once again share memories, introduce wives and girlfriends to shipmates and bid a final good-bye to the war. Many of the crew thought it a bittersweet occasion.

Manuel Mendez, torpedoman 3/c: "The decommissioning was both a sad and happy experience. We were young men who had the "Old Grey Lady" as our home for two years and more and the crew and officers as brothers and fathers to us all. In particular, the married amongst us were anxious to get home to our families and loved ones and get on with our lives."

The decommissioning party was the last time Pampanito's *crew was together. The war was over and most of them looked forward to returning to "normal" life. But this was one last chance to let go. The officers, top right, don't seem to be enjoying the party as much as the enlisted men. San Francisco Maritime National Park Association.*

Gordon Hopper, quartermaster 3/c: "It was alcohol-fueled chaos — enlisted men good-naturedly getting their evens with officers."

Clarence Williams, electrician's mate 2/c: "A lot of the regular crew had been transferred by then and it was kinda solemn; mixed emotions. Most of us knew we would be out soon and back home."

~~~

But *Pampanito*'s career wasn't over. Having done her part to win the war, she would become a landmark symbol of the Silent Service.

11

FROM MOTHBALLS
TO MUSEUM

Decommissioned on December 15, 1945 *Pampanito* was placed at Mare Island, California. The process of laying her up ("mothballing") began shortly after her final arrival in San Francisco and the removal of her torpedoes and supplies. It was a long, boring, tedious job for the crew.

Woodrow Weaver, CPO: "We had a lot of work to do in getting the old boat ready for retirement. All machinery had to be put in a state of preservation and many other things accomplished before she could be decommissioned."

Ona Hawkins, electrician's mate 3/c: "I helped prepare the boat for decommissioning, applying grease to gear and plastic cocoons to some equipment."

Spencer Stimler, radio technician 2/c: "The electronics that I was involved with were easily secured and from then on it was my job to take work parties to other subs in Mare Island. That was grunt work and so dirty that I managed to escape. I was supposed to stay with the work

parties but managed to outrank most of the bos'n mates that were in charge of the work details, so I just told them what to do while I went ashore."

One by one the crew departed, some returning to civilian life, others continuing their careers in the Navy. *Pampanito*, encased in plastic cocoons and covered with cosmoline and other preservatives, lay idle, water lapping at her sides. Completely sealed against the elements, she was pitch black inside while externally, her hull began accumulating marine growth below the water and rust above.

After fifteen years she was given a reprieve of sorts. In April of 1960 she was assigned as a training platform for Naval Reserve Submarine Division II-12 at Mare Island. Protective covering and coatings came off. Hatches were opened and the interior stale, dank atmosphere soon mixed with fresh air and sunshine. Some of her systems were energized for training and the crew's berthing area was stripped of

While a Naval Reserve training vessel at Mare Island, Pampanito, *right, was moored alongside* Sunfish SS-281. *San Francisco Maritime National Park Association.*

Once her Naval Reserve duty was over, Pampanito *was moored with the rest of the Navy's mothball fleet at Mare Island. Typically that marked the end of a valiant ship's career, but, in this case, it was the beginning of a new purpose in the boat's life. San Francisco Maritime National Park Association.*

its bunks to become a classroom. On November 6, 1962 she was reclassified as AGSS-383.[1]

    Pampanito remained part of the reserves until November 6, 1971 when she was found "unfit for further Naval service" and opened up to the fleet stripping program. Some of her machinery was removed to provide spare parts for other submarines. Later, authority was requested "to dispose of *Pampanito* … in a manner most advantageous to the government" and she was stricken from Navy records.

    Normally, this meant the boat would be sold to whichever ship dismantler offered the highest price. Once sold, she would be towed to a shipyard and cut into pieces. Her steel plates would be re-rolled and used in steel construction projects, possibly even ships, while her brass, copper and other metals would be melted down and re-manufactured.

    Fortunately, this would not be *Pampanito*'s fate. She had fallen under the eye of the San Francisco Maritime Museum.

---

[1] The prefix AG means Miscellaneous (auxilliary) in naval parlance.

The San Francisco Maritime National Park Association is a nonprofit organization dedicated to the study and preservation of maritime history. It began as the board of directors of the newly established San Francisco Maritime Museum in 1950. The museum's pride and main source of revenue was the three-masted sailing ship *Balclutha*. Berthed at San Francisco's Fisherman's Wharf, the ship was a major attraction to the public, evoking the city's long maritime heritage. During the three decades after the museum opened, it acquired the schooner *C.A. Thayer*, the steam schooner *Wapama*, the trans-Pacific sloop yacht *Mermaid*, the steam tug *Hercules* and the hay schooner *Alma*.

Unlike traditional museums, museum ships have extremely high, ongoing maintenance costs. They are constantly subjected to the effects of sun, wind and rain. Ships require constant upkeep to protect them against these elements. Because they are usually acquired after generations of neglect, additional funding is necessary to restore them to their original configuration.

It eventually became apparent that the admission charges for the museum, with the *Balclutha* the main attraction, were not enough to support what had become one of the largest museum fleets (in tonnage) in the world. Rather than fight a stubborn but losing battle, the Association donated the ships and its collections to the National Park Service, an agency of the federal government which had the funds to assure the ships' continued survival.

No longer directly responsible for the *Balclutha* or any of the other Hyde Street vessels, the Association suddenly found itself rudderless. It lacked an independent role in local maritime history. The board needed something on which to focus its energies and, more important, something to generate funds to expand the Association's activities and help ensure the daunting and costly task of preserving their former fleet of museum ships. The federal government could make sure the fleet survived, but the Association also wanted to be sure they were preserved in a manner that was historically accurate and attractive to the public.

Someone suggested a World War II submarine. The choice was logical because the Silent Service was a major factor in the war in the Pacific and Mare Island, in the north part of San Francisco Bay, had long been a U.S. Navy submarine construction and repair facility. In addition,

it was soon discovered that existing museum submarines were popular with the public, well-visited and generated more than enough income to cover maintenance and museum operation. Finally, the timing was near perfect. A submarine at Mare Island was about to be declared surplus by the Navy. And, having been a reserve training vessel, *Pampanito* was in excellent condition.

Inquiries were made of the Navy. They were receptive to the idea of her becoming a museum in San Francisco. All the Association had to do was sign the paperwork and take the boat to her new home. Where, exactly, that new home would be was yet to be determined.

Once assured the Navy would let them have the boat, the Museum Association began work on getting a good berth in San Francisco. They first approached the San Francisco Port Commission at their meeting of May 8, 1974. At that time Port Director Miriam E. Wolff suggested that Pier 41 might be the best location for the boat. David Nelson, assistant to the museum's board of trustees expressed the desire to berth her at Pier 45 at Fisherman's Wharf, which at that time was still used commercially although plans were to release the pier from "maritime use" in the near future. Nelson said that the Association would install railings, stairways, protective coverings for instruments and other gear and provide an entrance through the forward torpedo loading hatch and exit in the aft torpedo loading hatch.

As the first minor difficulties were overcome, the Association became optimistic. Their proposal went before the Bay Conservation and Development Commission (BCDC) on November 20, 1975. A BCDC permit was needed before the sub could be put on display. Commissioner Quentin Kopp tried to attach conditions to the permit because he was "concerned about tieing up Pier 45" by a long-term lease he was afraid the Port Commission might grant. He first amended the BCDC approval to say that the submarine museum must be in operation by December 31, 1976. That amendment passed. Then he tried to put an expiration date of December 31, 1977 with options for renewal. It looked as if this amendment, too, might pass. The Association wanted a longer commitment. Most of the board sided with Kopp. There was a lengthy debate and it wasn't until David Nelson pointed out that a short-term lease might jeopardize acquisition of the boat from the Navy, that fifteen

With a Navy tug alongside her port quarter, Pampanito *is prepared for the tow to Colberg's Ship Yard in Stockton. Originally it was planned for her to stay there a few months. She was there for six years. San Francisco Maritime National Park Association.*

votes of the commission swung the other way. The amendment was defeated and the motion passed; the permit was granted.

At this point the Association had been working on the project for three years. Nelson said he expected the boat to be turned over in February 1976 and it would take six months to prepare her for public display. They had no lease from the Port Commission at that time, but Nelson was assured such a matter would be routine. Part of his presentation to the BCDC was a letter from Port Director Thomas Soules assuring the museum that the east face of Pier 45 was available. Dated September 17, 1975, the letter read, in part, "… For now you are assured of the Pier 45 berth and of our continuing interest in providing the most advantageous berth for the *Pampanito*. Any assistance this office can give in expediting your projects which include historic vessels and berthing requests will be handled with pleasure and dispatch."

On May 1, 1976, while negotiations with the port continued, *Pampanito* was turned over to the National Maritime Museum Association.[1] She was immediately towed by Crowley tugs to Colberg shipyards in Stockton, California. There she would be made ready for the public and her promised berth at Fisherman's Wharf.

Taking possession of the boat was far easier than opening it up for public display. First, $110,000 was needed to renovate *Pampanito* to

---

[1] In August of 2000 the organization's name was changed to the San Francisco Maritime National Park Association.

Harry Bridges, right, president of the ILWU, came to prominence during the 1930s fighting for his union. He was equally outspoken in the 1970s against berthing Pampanito *at Fisherman's Wharf.* San Francisco Chronicle, *courtesy of San Francisco Maritime National Park Association.*

make her safe for the public. Funds were solicited from board members, many of whom were executives with San Francisco shipping companies. The Association's efforts ran into a wall of skepticism. Few of those approached believed the group's income projections for the submarine. Some board members felt that the concept of a maritime museum meant merchant marine history only, not Navy. Others were satisfied they had done their part in funding the *Balclutha* restoration.

Joseph Houghteling, chairman, NMMA publications committee: "The funds were eventually found in the Association's own earnings, mainly from the percentage of the *Balclutha* admissions we collected on behalf of the National Park Service."

However, the berth, previously assured, now became a major stumbling block. Harry Bridges, of the ILWU (International Longshoremen and Warehouseman's Union) and a member of the San Francisco Port Commission was dead set against it. Tom Richardson, Assistant Manager, USS *Pampanito*: "His politics were to the left and he did not really think that a war vessel was appropriate for the waterfront. He tried to make it out we were trying to glorify war, which was farthest from our minds, really."

As early as July 1, Bridges threatened to fight further attempts to berth the *Pampanito* by organizing peace groups to protest her display. Serving his last term as president of the ILWU he said he opposed the berthing of the sub at Fisherman's Wharf because he considered the vessel a "disgraceful symbol of war." His objection centered around the fact that, according to him, in 1944 *Pampanito* sank Japanese "troopships" carrying Australian and English prisoners of war.

Harry Bridges, of the ILWU (International Longshoremen and Warehouseman's Union) and member of the San Francisco Port Commission was dead set against it.

Others felt Bridges' reasons were more personal. His wife was Japanese and he was Australian. It was felt he disliked the project because *Pampanito* was involved with the sinking of a Japanese ship in which a number of Australians were killed.

Although he was born in Australia, Bridges denied that had anything to do with his opposition. "The fact that there were Australians aboard those ships has nothing to do with this. I am opposed as a matter of principle to use a war vessel strictly so the Maritime Museum can make money.

"It's too bad we don't have a hunk of that bomb we dumped on Hiroshima. That would be a real money maker."

The proposal to berth *Pampanito* at Pier 45 appeared on the Port Commission's calendar for consideration on July 28, 1976.

Before the vote, Bridges took on David Nelson, assistant director of the museum.

"What is the purpose of exhibiting the submarine?" asked the aging longshoreman.

"To put it out as a historical object, an object lesson in history."

Bridges replied that he opposed the plan because of the sinking of the transport carrying POWs and the museum's plan "to make dough" by exhibiting the sub.

The berthing proposal was defeated four to one. Some members of the Commission, influenced no doubt by Bridges, said that to open the

Pampanito was kept at an isolated berth at Colberg's shipyard in Stockton during the almost six years it took to win the berthing battle. *San Francisco Maritime National Park Association.*

submarine to the public would be a glorification of war and unsuitable for display at the Wharf. As a result, *Pampanito* stayed in Stockton where she remained for almost six years in storage as the debate continued.

While in Stockton, she was modified for public display. Tied up at Colberg's shipyard, the long process of reconditioning her and making her safe for the public, began. David Nelson: "[Wilton] Colberg's a prince. He has watched over the ship to see that it was properly protected and did much work on it."

Tom Richardson: "During that time the Navy was always sort of threatening, 'Well maybe we should take the thing back if you people can't do this.'

"And then other cities — Vallejo, Rio Vista, even as far up as Eureka — were making pitches to the Navy. 'Why don't you let us have this boat, we can put it on display for you, no problem.'

"Ultimately, the Navy realized that to have it on display in San Francisco would be the best thing for it."

Meanwhile, the conflict for a berth continued. Although Bridges fought the battle single-handed most of the time, he did manage to get some local press through the various peace organizations he allied with. The Women's International League for Peace and Freedom joined with Women for Peace to write Port Director Soules: "Our commitment is to educate for peace and not for war. We, therefore, urge your withdrawal of the proposal to exhibit the submarine as being totally inappropriate."

And from the East Bay Women for Peace to the Port Commission: "We strongly protest the exhibit of a war vehicle. We would rather urge that the exhibit be a peaceful symbol which would encourage trade with all countries."

Former captain of *Pampanito,* Admiral Paul Summers' reaction was, "I'm madder than hell. Picture the thing. It was our third war patrol. It was unrestricted war. It was a war and we sank ships."

David Nelson, assistant director of the Maritime Museum: "The Museum is an historical society. We believe *Pampanito* has great historical value. She is the last of her kind. When she is displayed at Fisherman's Wharf, the explanation of her career, if anything, will cause a repugnance to war, not a glorification of it. Her actions and the bravery of her crew do not deserve desecration, but rather the opportunity to teach

"Her actions and the bravery of her crew do not deserve desecration, but rather the opportunity to teach us the meanness — but at the same time, the realness — of what war is all about."
David Nelson

us the meanness — but at the same time, the realness — of what war is all about."

Paul Summers: "We had no idea they carried prisoners. That wouldn't have made a difference anyway. We attacked."

The general public, too, got involved. In a letter published in a San Francisco newspaper, E.E. Humphrey pointed out: "Some years ago San Francisco could have had the historical USS *California* and through bickering of petty politicos this never came about and the battleship *California* went to the highest bidder for scrap.

"Meanwhile North Carolina and Texas acquired the ships named after their states and converted them to museums with the thousands of tourists who came aboard more than paying for upkeep.

"Thousands of those of us who served on what Harry Bridges called "symbols of war" need no advice on what we should see or not see.

"No one is forcing the pacifists to board the *Pampanito*, and in no way should hinder those who wish to."

Beverly Bastian Meyers, honorary president of the Landmarks Society, put the issue into proper perspective. "Historical events can be judged fairly only in terms of the point in history in which they took place and the given conditions under which the people involved had to make decisions; it is never reasonable to make full judgement, good or bad, on hindsight or new standards of another time."

Adm. Summers remembered the attitude of the survivors: "Hell, no, the survivors weren't bitter toward us. I'll never forget it. I went up to the torpedo room and gave a little speech, and they sang, 'For He's a Jolly Good Fellow.' Even though most of their fellow prisoners drowned, it was because the Japanese wouldn't pick them up."

Yet, the San Francisco Women's International League for Peace and Freedom felt compelled to state: "We feel the vessel is an affront to the Japanese people, who are now our allies, and exhibits a callous insensitivity to the tragic loss of Australian and English prisoners. ... I think the American people are heartily sick of war and its reminders."

Eventually, Thomas Crowley, whose tugboats had been active in San Francisco Bay since the 19th century, entered the fray on the side of the Museum Association. His influence on the Port Commission was powerful. He convinced them that the boat would be a fitting monument to the city's maritime heritage and the horrors of war. Through his efforts

another vote was taken and on May 27, 1981 the San Francisco Port Commission voted four to one to allow the National Maritime Museum Association to display the *Pampanito* at Pier 45 as a memorial to those who died in the war and to raise money by charging a fee to tour the boat.

Afterward, Commissioner Dr. Authur Coleman said, "We should not hide our past. History is open to all. If we've made mistakes, we should make sure we do not repeat them."

Chris Bach, manager, USS *Pampanito*: "Both the port commissioners and the San Francisco supervisors said that they didn't want an object that was a glorification of war on the waterfront. And it took them six years to say that this was not a glorification of war but a memorial to those who served."

Harry Bridges, however, was not graceful in defeat, stating "We promised that World War II would be an end to war. We promised then we would have a world of peace. This cheapens the reputation of those who fought and died in World War II."

March 11, 1982 and Pampanito *leaves the Stockton Deep Water Channel Turning Basin en route to her new berth at Pier 45 in San Francisco. She was towed by the Crowley tugs* Trojan, *left, and* Sea Fox. *The Stockton Record, courtesy of San Francisco Maritime National Park Association.*

Nonetheless, the vote was final. With what was considered the major hurdle overcome, there remained the process of getting permission from the Bay Conservation and Development Commission and several other agencies. These quickly fell into place. Finally, after six long years, the Association's submarine would have a berth.

Pampanito made the voyage from Stockton to Pier 45 on March 11, 1982. She was opened to the public four days later. Opening ceremonies were attended by Mayor Dianne Feinstein and Admiral Paul Summers, former captain of *Pampanito.*

Now the question was, would the public be interested. Were the Association's projections correct? Would *Pampanito* generate enough money to maintain the ships of the National Maritime Historical Park, or would she be a massive white elephant, destined once more for the scrap yard?

Tom Richardson: "There was some real fear, what if this thing just goes south on us? What are we going to do with it then?"

12

RESTORATION

Welcomed by an enthusiastic public, *Pampanito* was an immediate success. What was feared might be a white elephant turned out to be a golden goose. In 1983, the submarine's first full year of operation, the National Maritime Museum Association's income was $808,925 with a net of $312,116. This compares with a 1981 (the last full year before she opened) income of $264,740 and a net of $27,744.

It was clear early on that funding would not be a problem. But there remained the difficult task of preserving *Pampanito*, restoring her to her wartime configuration and interpreting her role in history to the public.

Tom Richardson, Assistant Manager: "Basic questions had to be addressed: do we need a crew of deckhands, who's going to take care of the lines, who's going to make sure we've got our chaffing gear out, and what are they going to do if there's problems with the gangway."

What was needed was someone with a passion for the boat, someone with an all-consuming desire to see her restored to as near operational status as possible, and with all her systems functioning as they did in World War II.

It was then that Russell Booth came on the scene. He was exactly the right person for the job. It was as if he and the boat were meant for each other.

Tom Richardson: "Russ was the driving force behind really establishing a crew here at *Pampanito* because he realized we needed to take care of the boat. When Russ came aboard he had to address all these problems. He made the case that we needed to build a crew of people who are going to be here, reliable, around the clock, seven days a week; expanding that crew.

Russell Booth, Pampanito *'s guiding light during her second life, shown after a hard day's restoration. San Francisco Maritime National Park Association.*

"He realized we need a twenty four hour watch on the boat, just to make sure nothing happens at night or make sure that nobody hops the fence, all those different things. The board was willing to spend the money but they needed to be certain it would be money well-spent.

Charles A. McGuire, original crewman: "Russ Booth did a fabulous job. Nobody else could have done a job like this. I used to think

"Russ was the driving force behind really establishing a crew here at Pampanito *because he realized we needed to take care of the boat."*

Tom Richardson

Although taken circa 1985-87, this photo is representative of how Pampanito *looked jst after after arrival at her new berth at Pier 45: no guns and no number yet painted on the conning tower. San Francisco Maritime National Park Association.*

I could do that, but there's no way that I would have made that boat look as beautiful as Russ Booth and his crew have."

Al MacDonald, volunteer: "Russell Booth was a big part of this. He was just extremely interested in restoration of ships. I understand that the *Pampanito* is, of the fifteen submarines that we have around the country, probably in the best shape of any of them."

Earl Watkins, original crewmember: "Russell Booth did so much to restore the *Pampanito*; she was his pride and joy."

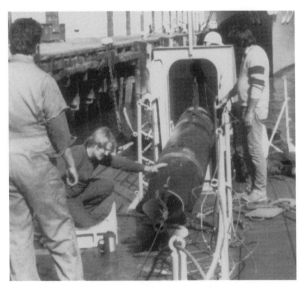

Restoring the boat included laying in a supply of unarmed torpedoes through the companionways. San Francisco Maritime National Park Association.

"Russ Booth did a fabulous job. Nobody else could have done a job like this."

Charles A. McGuire

Russell Booth's determination in restoring Pampanito *is shown by the "Don't give up the ship" flag in the Pier 45 workshed area alongside the boat. San Francisco Maritime National Park Association.*

Day-to-day safety of *Pampanito* and her visitors was but one of the early problems that were overcome. There was also the need to restore the boat to her wartime status. This, too, required perseverance and vision. Tom Richardson: "One of the most important things that Russ accomplished in those early years, he convinced the board that *Pampanito* could be more than a static display. We had to develop it as an exhibit, try and restore it because *Pampanito* wasn't in the condition she's in today. It was quite a bit different. He made the case to create budgets that could be used to preserve what we've got and make acquisitions so we can restore systems and compartments on board the boat. That's probably Russ's biggest legacy. He really put it on the path to becoming one of the best restored World War II naval vessels afloat. Which I think it is."

In the years since she opened to the public, *Pampanito* has been under a program of constant restoration and acquisition. Even while various areas of the boat are routinely preserved against the elements and the erosion of time, parts and equipment are acquired to bring her appearance to the way it was in 1945. That year was chosen because of modifications made to the boat after her last wartime patrol. Tom Richardson explains: "That point in time is pretty much dictated by *Pampanito*'s exterior structure. In May of '45 she returned to Hunter's Point for a final refit. She was going to head out for the planned invasion of Japan which was going to be November of that year. But that never happened. Those circles [on the photographs, see previous chapter] are where they added the SV or the Sugar Victor radar which is an air search

"That's probably Russ's biggest legacy. He really put it on the path to becoming one of the best restored World War II naval vessels afloat."

Tom Richardson

Here, the boat sports a coat of primer, prior to painting. Note the cruiser gun and the radar antenna mast added at Hunter's Point in 1945. San Francisco Maritime National Park Association.

radar. That's that big ol' mast, hydraulically driven, and that was going to be of some use in patrolling close off the coast of Japan. When that was installed, that pretty much dictated the period you had to restore it to because that's still there today. It's one of the biggest features there on the cigarette deck.

Al MacDonald: "You've got two radars up there. You've got a surface and an aerial. Line of sight type of stuff, twenty-five miles, whatever."

Tom Richardson: "So, we set that point at the summer of 1945. That's the point in time we're trying to restore it to. We're very fortunate because *Pampanito* escaped a lot of post war modification because she remained in the mothball fleet for fifteen years and still has the original bow; the conning tower was not streamlined. The guns were removed but all the foundations are still there. So it was just a matter of locating guns and reinstalling them — of course that was easier said than done!"

That they were doing things correctly was proven when, in 1986, *Pampanito* was declared a National Historic Landmark.

National Historic Landmark status came in 1986. Author.

Through the years the Association slowly acquired most of the equipment and armament needed to bring the boat to that point in 1945 when she was refitted at Hunter's Point. In some cases, such as the main deck gun, they installed what was available (although not accurate) for the sake of overall appearance while the search continued for the original equipment. Tom Richardson: "When we first got it we had no deck guns whatsoever. They wanted to put something up there just to fill the space so they got a five-inch deck gun said to be from the cruiser *Los Angeles* which was scrapped down in Long Beach. That was brought up here and put on the forward deck and, to probably seventy-five percent of our visitors, they didn't realize it was the wrong gun. But we knew it was not a wet mount submarine gun. We always hoped that someday we could acquire a real submarine gun.

"In 1990 we made contact with a group in Michigan that had the gun we have now, the Manistee Clan Muzzleloaders Gun Club. They

The 4-inch submarine gun came from a muzzle-loaders club in Michigan. Not only authentic, it was historic, coming from the fleet sub Tautog. *San Francisco Maritime National Park Association.*

were using it to muzzle load and firing it off in this field up in Manistee, Michigan. We asked them if they'd like to make a trade. We told them, 'We have this five-inch gun from the cruiser *Los Angeles* that's much, much bigger than that four-inch gun you got.'

"They said something like, 'Oh, sure, sure, we'll trade.' They liked the idea of getting a bigger gun.

"We effected the trade and brought this gun here and it turned out that this gun was actually from the submarine *Tautog* which was one of the highest scoring subs of World War II. It's not only an authentic four-inch submarine deck gun, it's historic too.

"We paid all the transportation costs and what-have-you to get this gun back here. We completely disassembled it, removed all the rust and scale and crummy paint and everything and started from the ground up. We had a manual to work from which was helpful. We completely re-coated it and put it back together. It doesn't fire, there's no firing pin, but it's closer to operation than when we got it. It's in much better condition.

"All that takes a little bit of money, of course. But, more important, it takes manpower, it takes people who have a love for this ship to pursue these things. We had been looking for a deck gun for years and we probably should have just given up. But we didn't. And after we had been open eight or nine years we found the right one."

The other deck guns came from other museum ships and the Navy. The first 20mm gun was donated from the submarine USS *Bowfin* exhibit in Hawaii. They had extra guns in their (*continued on page 160*)

The 20mm guns came from the USS Bowfin *and the U.S. Navy. Author.*

"It turned out that this gun was actually from the submarine Tautog *which was one of the highest scoring subs of World War II. It's not only an authentic four-inch submarine deck gun, it's historic, too."*

Tom Richardson

DRYDOCKING

All ships, boats and submarines must be taken out of the water periodically. Generally, drydocking provides a chance to clean marine growth off a vessel, paint the hull to protect it against salt water corrosion and renew the sacrificial anodes that protect the hull against electrolysis. Sometimes this is referred to as "a shave and a haircut." It also is an opportunity to make repairs to the underwater portion of the hull and any fittings that go through the hull. *Pampanito* is on a six- to seven-year drydocking schedule and has been drydocked in 1986, 1993 and 1999.

Clockwise from upper left: Pampanito *and drydock at Oakland; welding on propeller strut; whalelike view of stern after painting; barnacles and marine growth just after haulout; welding lower portion of hull. San Francisco Maritime National Park Association.*

Above, Pampanito *after painting and before gangway is removed. Below, just prior to flooding of the drydock. The steel box suspended in the center of the photo is how the crew gets aboard at this point. Above, George Bonawit, below, San Francisco Maritime National Park Association.*

THE WASHING MACHINE

An example of the difficulties and complications in acquiring items was *Pampanito*'s washing machine. Tom Richardson describes the organization's frustrations in getting one. "We had been looking for a washing machine, really since Day One. We knew what kind we wanted. I never really thought we were ever going to find one. Then we were out at Pearl Harbor two years ago [in 1997] for the Historic Naval Ships Conference and the superintendent of the INACSHIPFAC (INACtive SHIP FACility) made it available for us to go out to the ships that were out there. We found that washing machine! We did all the paperwork and were able to get it. But even then it wasn't a done deal because when we first earmarked it, they said, 'Sure, no problem.' Then when they sent their people out to tag it for removal, they said, 'Oh, well it's coated with cosmoline and some PCB based preservatives, I don't think you can have it.'

"We said, 'Well, gosh, what do we have to do to make this happen?'

"They said, 'Well, you'd have to have it cleaned up at a facility and oh, gee, our facility here will do it but it's going to cost you ten thousand dollars.'

"Finally one of our volunteers, Richard Pekelney, really dogged this. He wrote a number of letters to the different people from the Navy and found out exactly what was needed to get it cleaned up. We got permission to do the clean up here at our end if they would simply shrink-wrap it and ship it to us. So we had it all cleaned up by people who are qualified to handle hazardous materials and they were disposed of properly and we were able to get it shipped here. We first made contact with them back in October of '97 and didn't get it until April or May of this year, '99, over a year and a half, I'd say, before we finally got it. And several points along the way we thought it just wasn't going to happen. We were getting a lot of 'no's.'"

(*continued from page 157)* inventory and were pleased to donate one to *Pampanito*. Other 20mm's came from the Navy. The 40mm gun was discovered at a Naval storage annex in Virginia by one of the boat's former crewmembers. Inquiries were made to the Naval Historical Center which agreed to let the *Pampanito* organization have it on loan. After cleaning and repainting it looked like new. The gunmounts for the 20mm came from the [Liberty Ship] *Jeremiah O'Brien*.

Pampanito's 40mm gun came from a Naval storage annex in Virginia. Author.

Typical of the challenges and creativity in restoring the boat was the difficulty in recreating the crew's berthing space. Tom Richardson: "The crew's berthing was completely stripped out and was used as a classroom space for the Naval Reserve. We had always hoped that we could find bunks. That's one of the reasons that we went up to [the National Defense Reserve Fleet at] Suisun Bay all those times. We were looking for bunks that would be approximately what *Pampanito* had. They just didn't have'em aboard any of those ships. We were able to strip out the webbing from a lot of those bunks up there, off those Victory ships and finally, what we ended up doing, was having the frames fabricated over in the East Bay at an iron shop; fabricated to match the few originals that we had. We installed the webbing on those. The mattresses were donated by a sub that was being overhauled up at Mare Island. We had the flash covers manufactured by an upholstery company locally.

"Again, it took people persevering to do the job, to get the work done. Also, it took money. That's one of the good things about *Pampanito*, the money's been there for the most part. And a lot of it had to do with the location. We have to follow that fundamental rule of real estate value — location, location, location. To be here at Fisherman's Wharf is really a big help to the submarine. But we are a nonprofit organization and we can't just spend freely. We have to be measured in the projects we want to bite off and make sure the funds are there. And that's probably one of the bigger stories of *Pampanito* over the last eighteen years, people identifying what needs to be restored, developing a plan to do it and pursuing it.

The movie studio made it financially worthwhile for Pampanito *to turn away her public for a few weeks. San Francisco Maritime National Park Association.*

"Sometimes it's frustrating. Just because you decide to do something doesn't mean it's going to happen, next month or even next year. Sometimes these things take years to come to fruition. And it's important not to lose hope."

In the Spring of 1995 *Pampanito* left her berth to "star" in the feature film *Down Periscope. Pampanito* played the fictitious submarine USS *Stingray* SS-161. (The real USS *Stingray* was hull number SS-186 and SS-161 was the *S-50.*) It was an interesting interlude for both the *Pampanito* crew and 20th Century Fox.

Left, the film crew paints Pampanito's *deck as part of her conversion to* Stingray. *Above, note the "Hollywood" effect on the boat aft of the gangway. She looks well-used and slightly decrepit. San Francisco Maritime National Park Association.*

For its part, Fox was delighted to have the sub. Michael Corenblith, production designer: "The *Pampanito* is the quintessential World War II submarine. It is sort of a classic car in that everything we associate with those submarines is contained within the *Pampanito* and her experiences.

A member of the film crew puts the finishing touches on Pampanito's *new emblem as* Stingray. *San Francisco Maritime National Park Association.*

It's like something out of a film like 'Run Silent, Run Deep' or 'Operation Pacific.'"

The boat was towed to the Suisun Bay Reserve Fleet which served as a Navy Base. Michael Corenblith: "We found that in the water off of

Although it looks like Pampanito *is under her own power, she is actually being pulled by a tugboat toward the Golden Gate Bridge. This is how 20th Century Fox made it look as if the boat were underway. Robert Taylor, San Francisco Maritime National Park Association.*

With the excitement of her movie debut complete, Pampanito *returned to her berth at Pier 45. Even before removing the* Stingray *logo, she was again open to the public. San Francisco Maritime National Park Association.*

the city of Benicia was a tremendous surface fleet held in readiness by the Department of Transportation. They weren't really mothballed, but there in case of emergency. We were able to work among these ships without having to involve the military. We built a dock by linking several barges together, giving us the illusion of a land-based naval dock surrounded by ships."

Bob Taylor, volunteer: "We lived on the submarine with the rest of them. We would stay over night and we'd get all that good food. We would get the leftovers. We would go up about 3 o'clock and have cold prime rib and all this stuff laying around at night. We all got fat. We would stay on board about four or five days and then go home. Most of it was made up in Suisun Bay. We were tied up there.

"I was more enchanted by the talent of the crew, the electricians and the key grips and these guys. They were just so talented. They could just build anything. They'd make a storm at night with nothing but lights and wind machines. They're using beautiful plywood, paint it, not a single knot in it. We had a great time with them."

Even Kelsey Grammer, the star, was affected by *Pampanito*'s aura. "It was like a costume drama in a way. I changed my hair, trimmed down a little bit, put on the uniform. But you get on to that boat, you start to walk a little differently. I started to assume the gestures of command. But what really went through my mind was the enormous commitment the men made who served on it. It gave me a great sense of respect and duty as well as appreciation for their sacrifices."

Bob Taylor: "Kelsey Grammer, we all liked him. He was very friendly."

One of the more unexpected aspects of making the movie was how tedious the process could be. Bob Taylor: "It was nothing really, besides just watching it. Russ Booth was our manager and he came up with the expression that watching them make movies is like watching paint dry. Hour after hour of the same thing. They do it over and over again."

Although restoration of *Pampanito* was planned with a very definite purpose in mind, to bring her as close to her 1945 configuration as possible, the process had an unexpected benefit. It brought about the development of an overnight program, and with (*continued on page 168*)

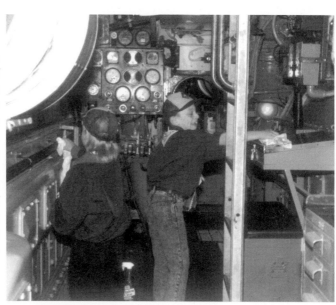

Opening the boat to scouting groups and school children gives them the opportunity to study submarines and learn history. Here cub scouts from Pack 383, Fremont, help spruce up the boat for a Memorial Day ceremony. San Francisco Maritime National Park Association.

"*What really went through my mind was the enormous commitment the men made who served on it. It gave me a great sense of respect and duty as well as appreciation for their sacrifices.*"

Kelsey Grammer

REUNIONS

Pampanito represents many things to many people. To tourists, ship aficionados and school children she provides an opportunity to learn about submarine operation and the glory and horror that was World War II. But to her former crew and the POWs she rescued, she is much more than that. *Pampanito* was their home, their very existence for days, weeks and months. She encapsulates all the camaraderie, joy, sorrow, excitement and boredom of that distant war. Within the confines of her steel structure they felt the heady excitement of victory, were brushed by death and shared in the simple fact that they survived. It is no wonder that reunions are special events to these people, a time to renew old acquaintances, share war stories, laugh and perhaps shed a few tears for those that can no longer make it.

The first reunion was in 1985 and attended by Adm. Summers. Others have been held since then and now the former crew meets about every two years in San Francisco.

One special reunion was Austrailia's award of its "Defense Force" plaque to Pampanito. *Clock-wise from bottom right: Frank Farmer, the first POW pulled out of the water; Adm. Summers, with Frank and other POWs, and his eloquent remembrance at the museum. San Francisco Maritime National Park Association.*

Reunions are a chance for a group photo on the "old boat" ...

And later there's always the special cake and another photo at the party afterward.

A reunion of another type involves current volunteers and staff. Here gathered aboard for a special breakfast, they share stories of the boats and ships they were on, their experiences during various wars, and, occasionally, pause for a moment or two of quiet reflection. San Francisco Maritime National Park Association.

Children and Scouts spend part of their time aboard Pampanito *learning how she operates. San Francisco Maritime National Park Association.*

(*continued from page 165*) it, a new way to open up the boat to school children — and an unexpected new revenue source to support her ongoing restoration. Tom Richardson: "It really started out as kind of a fun camping exercise. One of the members of the Naval Reserve unit that used to drill down here back in the late '80s was involved with a Boy Scout troop up in Vallejo. He asked if they could bring a group for an overnight stay back in '88 or '89. So we said, 'O.K, sure.' We didn't have any bunks aboard at that time and we didn't charge anything. We just let them bring their group and they spent the night. And they continued to do this on an annual basis. Then more and more Boy Scout groups were hearing about this and they would bring their groups.

Many of the scouts become quite serious when it comes to learning submarine operation. San Francisco Maritime National Park Association.

Assistant Manager Tom Richardson, left, and volunteer Al MacDonald, during an infrequent coffee break. Author.

"After a while we started thinking, there may be a business here. Plus we were finding out that, indeed, other ships around the country were having overnight encampments and they were actually charging money for it and it was becoming a major source of revenue. So we decided we should probably start planning the same thing. But we didn't have bunks on board the submarine. We had to go through that process of restoring the crew's berthing space and once we did that in 1993 we officially launched the *Pampanito* overnight program as an education program. In February of 1994 we started our first groups that paid to spend the night.

"I was concerned initially that we were going to have a lack of interest because what was previously free we were now charging for. But we started to add a few more things to the tour — going to see the conning tower, getting close up to a torpedo tube or seeing the radio room and things like that, things we weren't doing before. As it turned out there was no fall off in interest, in fact it increased. We went from forty or so groups the first year to close to 200 groups a year now.

Chris Bach, manager, *Pampanito*: "We run about 6000 kids and parents in the overnight education program where we bring the kids in, we introduce them to the association of the *Pampanito*, tell them a little about submarine history and how a submarine operates and then go more into the detail of how the *Pampanito* served in the war through its war patrols and its history and then they get to spend the night aboard. They sleep in the crew's berthing area and officers' country. We have a

"We run about 6000 kids and parents in the overnight program, tell them a little about submarine history and how a submarine operates and then go more into the detail of how the Pampanito *served in the war through its war patrols and its history."*
Chris Bach

The overnight program allows youngsters to sleep in crew bunks aboard Pampanito. *It has grown to the point where groups are booked a year in advance. San Francisco Maritime National Park Association.*

capacity of forty-eight overnight guests at one time. That's the maximum.

"For the weekends we're booked over a year in advance. It's been a very successful program. We're getting groups from as far north as Redding and as far south as Santa Barbara and Ventura County."

Tom Richardson: "We've continued to enhance the program and give it more structure and make it more educational. The kids learn the rudimentary history of the *Pampanito* plus they learn the basics of how a submarine operates. We take them through the boat and explain things on board and down in the control room. They take our audio tour and we take them up in the conning tower. By the end of the night they really have learned quite a bit about submarines, more than they realize. Then we have them test this themselves. We provide them a worksheet which the kids work on when they stand watches at night. And the worksheet really shows how much they learned. It's become quite an educational program."

As *Pampanito* came into the twenty-first century, her educational program continues to develop. In addition to overnight stays, special day tours are planned for school children of all ages. Tom Richardson: "We realize that if we want to grow our educational programs we need to reach out to schools more, because we're getting very few school groups now."

Chris Bach: "We offer our current day programs to the San Francisco School District for $2 per person — basically a briefing of the submarine and the same audio tour given to the general public. We also received a grant to subsidize youth groups for our overnight program"

Tom Richardson: "We're going to offer a program which dovetails with what the kids need to learn. We've learned the hard way that you just can't make up a program and expect people to come. You need to have the teachers sign off initially to kind of help you develop it so that it meets their needs. Teachers are more and more being pressed upon to teach certain standards and there are set standards in California for social sciences, for science, math, and so on."

Chris Bach: "This summer [1999] we got together with the San Francisco School District. They supplied four middle school teachers, science teachers, who decided how they could best utilize our facility to perform their course curriculum."

Tom Richardson: "We looked at the science framework for the State of California and identified some teaching elements for their classes which can be explained very well by the *Pampanito*. Everything that makes her operate is a science-based process. So we're going to have an educational program which exhibits some of those science processes in kind of a fun way with hands-on activity. This would involve everything from sonar to optics with periscopes, chemical batteries, things of that nature. We're going to have basically a typical seventh or eighth grade class with about thirty-six kids spend the night in the submarine and they'll work through five different science stations doing rotation and complete a log book as they go through. At the end of the night we'll see who's been most accurate with their recorded results and they'll receive an award."

Chris Bach: "That curriculum has now been approved by both our education council, which is a combination of the school district and our trustees, and that's also gone to the San Francisco School District and it's been approved. They'll be starting those trial programs as each of those instructors will bring their own class. Once they work the program, they'll make some changes and massage the curriculum to see how it really works and then they plan on putting it into full swing. Hopefully we can maximize our nights during the school year, whereas with the

overnight program for the summer we're basically maxed to the hilt already."

Tom Richardson: "We don't want Pampanito to remain static. We want it to become more involved with the community it serves right here in San Francisco by doing these educational programs. In that way we can have whole generations of school children who can say, 'I remember the *Pampanito*, I spent the night on her, we learned something, we had a lot of fun there.' They become part of our constituency and hopefully if they stay in the Bay Area they'll think about us. They'll bring their families back to visit us or if we ever need support in Congress or with the Maritime Park, it will be something they remember. Or maybe they'll stay with us as members of our organization. So, it's critical that we do this.

"I think that it is critical in the life of any historic ship to make herself invaluable to the community she serves. If they don't try to do something to engage the community they serve, they're ultimately just going to become a rusty hull that's going to be forgotten about. Nobody's going to go to bat for them when their berth is threatened or developers come in and want to push it aside or some people declare it to be an eyesore, whatever. You've got to keep the history alive, the science alive, for the community, so that people say, 'No, that's valuable. We need that.' And that's what we want to do with *Pampanito*."

Since *Pampanito* opened, the National Maritime Museum Association has worked to interpret the vessel to her visitors and to preserve and restore her to her wartime condition and appearance. Most of the equipment that was missing when the boat was acquired has been replaced. *Pampanito* has been drydocked three times by the Association and she is on a regular haul-out schedule of about six years. Many of *Pampanito's* systems have been brought back to life and made operational as part of her extensive preservation program. Three of the diesel engines are in running condition and the galley is operational, to name just a few of the projects being worked on. The effort continues seven days a week.

And it comes as no surprise to those who believed in the project that the submarine not only pays her own way, but helps maintain the other ships at the San Francisco Maritime National Historical Park. After

"We can have whole generations of school children who can say, 'I remember the Pampanito, *I spent the night on her, we learned something, we had a lot of fun there.'"*

Tom Richardson

setting aside enough money for operations, restoration and a dry-docking reserve, there is still enough (25 cents of every revenue dollar) for other maritime history projects. Among these have been decking for the *Balclutha,* a grant to the SS *Jeremiah O'Brien,* sails for the *Alma,* acquisition of the Alfred Palmer films on Pacific Coast shipping lines, Nimitz lectures at the University of California, restoration of the *China* cabin, San Francisco's Festival of the Sea and Fleet Week.

~~~

Submarines changed a great deal after World War II. The replacement of the diesel engines with nuclear power created radical changes in hull design. Boats became larger, faster and are able to stay submerged indefinitely. For example, the Ohio-class submarine carries 24 ballistic missiles, measures 560 feet long and has a nuclear reactor that develops 35,000 horsepower. This compares to *Pampanito*'s ten torpedo tubes, a length of 312 feet and four diesel engines developing a total of 5,400 horsepower. No longer "submersible boats," today's vessels are true submarines.

But the more telling difference is in the appearance. Modern submarines, large, round, dark and sleek, have been described as looking like "happy whales." The World War II fleet submarine looked exactly like what it was — a steel shark. And those that sailed them will tell you the appearance represented the character of the boat: menacing, powerful, formidable.

The Golden Gate Bridge as seen through Pampanito's *periscope. San Francisco Maritime National Park Association.*

APPENDICES
BIBLIOGRAPHY
ABOUT THE AUTHOR
INDEX

APPENDIX A
USS PAMPANITO
SS-383
SPECIFICATIONS

Built by Portsmouth Naval Shipyard, Portsmouth, New Hampshire.

Keel laid: March 15, 1943
Launched: July 12, 1943
Commissioned: November 6, 1943
Displacement:
   surfaced: 1,525 tons
   submerged: 2,415 tons
Length overall: 311 ft. 9 in.
Beam: 27 ft. 3 in.
Draft: 15 ft. 8 in.
Pressure Hull: 7/8 in. high tensile steel
Main Engines: Four Fairbanks-Morse 10-cylinder opposed piston.
Total horsepower:
   5,400 surfaced
   2,740 submerged
Main generator: Elliot
Generator power:
   1,120 kw @ 720 rpm
   900 kw @ 650 rpm

Maximum speed:
   surfaced: 21 knots
   submerged: 11 knots
Cruising range:
   surfaced: 22,000 miles
   submerged: 95 miles at 5 knots
Endurance: 70 days
Operating depth: 400 ft.
Armament: 10 torpedo tubes (6 forward, 4 aft)
   One 4"/50 main deck gun
   Two 40mm guns
   Two 20mm guns

Propulsion Plant Details

Main engines. The four main diesel engines are opposed piston 38D-8 1/8-in. two-cycle. Opposed piston engines have two pistons for each cylinder, connected to crankshafts at the bottom and top of the engine. As the pistons move toward each other, air in the cylinder is compressed, fuel is injected and the resultant combustion pushes the pistons apart, rotating the crankshafts. The crankshafts are connected by a vertical drive gear.

Auxiliary engine. One 7-cylinder Fairbanks-Morse opposed piston 35A-5¼-in diesel.

Main generators. One of each of the four main generators is connected to each diesel engine. A single main generator or any combination of them can be used to charge the main storage batteries or power the main propulsion motors.

Auxiliary generator. One Elliot generator rated at 300 kw. The auxiliary generator, powered by the auxiliary engine, supplies power for all auxiliary circuits, charges the main storage batteries at a low rate or can be used to power the main propulsion motors through the batteries.

Batteries. Two 126-cell storage batteries. Each cell is 15 in. deep, 21 in. wide, 54 in. tall and weighs 1,650 pounds. Each cell is made up of positive and negative plates made of lead, each with common terminals, separated by insulators. The plates are immersed in an electrolyte solution made up of pure water and pure sulfuric acid with a specific gravity of 1.250 when fully charged. Each cell produces approximately two volts and is permanently wired in series. Each of the two battery groups could be operated independently or in parallel. The batteries could deliver approximately 5,320 amps for one hour, 930 amps for ten hours or 235 amps for forty-eight hours. This means that the submarine could travel submerged at 11 knots for one hour or ninety-five miles at a speed of 5 knots before voltage falls to a limiting range.

Pampanito Kill List

Date	Vessel	Type	Tonnage	Location
9/12/44	*Kachidoki Maru*	Passenger-cargo	10,509	Marianas
9/12/44	*Zuiho Maru*	Oiler	5,135	Marianas
11/18/44	*Banshu Maru No. 17*	Auxiliary supply	459	Luzon Strait
11/18/44	*Shinko Maru*	Cargo	1,200	Luzon Strait
2/6/45	*Engen Maru*	Oiler	6,900	South China Sea
2/6/45	*Eifuku Maru*	Auxiliary gunboat	3,520	South China Sea
	Total Tonnage		27,723	

Appendix B

Officers and Men at Commissioning

6 November 1943

Officers

Lt. Cdr. Charles B. Jackson, Jr.,
  Commanding Officer
Lt. Cdr. Paul E. Summers, Executive Officer
Lt. Landon L. Davis
Lt. William H. McClaskey, Jr.
Lt. Clifford C. Grommet
Lt(jg). Francis M. Fives
Mm(t) James S. Heist

Enlisted

Agnello, Lewis Jerry
Aimone, Otto Peter, Jr.
Arcemont, Norman John
Attaway, Ralph Winston
Bacskay, Albert Joseph
Baron, Leonard

Bennett, Robert
Bienkowski, Chester Charles
Bobb, Louis Edward
Boozer, James Steadman
Bouchard, Jacques Florian
Branch, Lamont
Brown, George Valentine
Brown, Hubert Nelson
Connelly, William Guy
Cordon, Walter Harold
Costello, Irving Francis
Cox, James Elton
Currier, Andrew Louis
Davenport, Bartlett Nathaniel
De Buono, J-Uagindo
Eichner, Joseph Frederick
Ferguson, Donald Innes
George, Howard Edwin
Glazik, Henry John
Grady, William Christopher

179

Hauptman, Anthony Carl
Herber, Ralph Monroe
Hill, Mervin
Hill, Samuel Richard
Hopper, Gordon Lewis
Kaup, Norbert Anthony
King, Theodas Cowen, Jr.
Kordich, Nickolas
Kubacki, Edwin
Langin, Lawrence Harold
Lederer, Frank Joseph
Lombardi, Renard Joseph
MacVane, Lloyd Vivian
Madaras, John George
Matheny, Robert Joseph
McGuire, Charles Albert, Jr.
Merryman, William Walter
Meyers, Milton Alfred
Michno, Frank Ben
Moffett, George Edward
Moore, Melvin Henry

Morrow, William Franklin, Jr.
Mosey, Ray George
O'Neill, John Bernard
Pappas, Paul, Jr.
Partridge, Leland Root
Penn, Leonard Thomas
Rahner, Harold Joseph
Robinson, Isaac Frederick
Schilling, John Beveridge
Smith, John Franklin
Smith, Wendall Tyng
Stinson, Harry
Thaxton, O'Neal
Tonkin, Edward Martin
Van Atta, Albert Dillon, Jr.
Vaughan, Ishamel Worth
Watkins, Earl Finley
Weaver, Woodrow Wilson
Wilkerson, Jack Roslyn
Wilson, John Edward
Zalusky, Bernard

APPENDIX C

PERSONNEL ON THE FIRST WAR PATROL

15 March to 2 May 1944

Officers

Lt. Cdr. Paul Edward Summers, Commanding Officer

Lt. Landon Leslie Davis, Jr., Executive Officer and Navigator

Lt. William Harrison McClaskey, Jr., Engineering and Electrical Officer

Lt. Clifford Charles Grommett, First Lieutenant

Lt(jg). Edward Joseph Hannon, Jr., Torpedo and Gunnery Officer

Lt(jg). William Lee Bruckart, Radar Officer

Lt(jg). Francis Michael Fives, Communications Officer

Ens. John West Red, Jr., Commissary Officer

Mac. James Samuel Heist, Assistant Engineering Officer

Elect. Percy Bryan Pike, Assistant Electrical Officer

Enlisted

Agnello, Lewis Jerry
Aimone, Otto Peter, Jr.
Arcemont, Norman John
Attaway, Ralph Winston
Austin, Joseph Charles Cave
Bacskay, Albert Joseph
Baron, Leonard
Beaulieu, Laurent
Behney, James Harris
Bennett, Robert
Bobb, Louis Edward
Bouchard, Jacques Florian
Bourgeois, Roger Norman
Branch, Lamont
Brown, Duncan
Brown, Hubert Nelson

Canty, William Stephen
Carmody, Clarence George
Chinn, Harold
Cordon, Walter Harold
Costello, Irving Francis
Currier, Andrew Lewis
Davenport, Bartlett Nathaniel
Eberhard, Robert Earl
Eichner, Joseph Frederick
Ferguson, Donald Innes
George, Howard Edwin
Glazik, Henry John
Grady, William Christopher
Hauptman, Anthony Carl
Herber, Ralph Monroe
Hill, Mervin
Hopper, Gordon Lewis
Ingram, George
Kaup, Norbert Anthony
King, Theodas Cowen, Jr.
Kordich, Nickolas
Kubacki, Edwin
Langin, Lawrence Harold
Large, Bonham Davis
Lederer, Frank Joseph
Lombardi, Renard Joseph
MacVane, Lloyd Vivian
Madaras, John George
Martin, Lynn Leonard

Matheny, Robert Joseph
Mc Collum, William Henry
Mc Guire, Charles Albert, Jr.
Merryman, William Walter
Meyers, Milton Alfred
Michno, Frank Ben
Moffett, George Edward
Moore, Melvin Henry
Morrow, William Franklin, Jr.
Mosey, Ray George
O'Neill, John Bernard
Pappas, Paul, Jr.
Payton, Albert, Jr.
Rahner, Harold Joseph
Richter, Walter Herman
Robinson, Isaac Frederick
Schilling, John Beveridge
Smith, Clarence Harold
Smith, Wendall Tyng, Jr.
Stockslader, Edmund William
Tonkin, Edward Martin
Van Atta, Albert Dillon, Jr.
Walters, Roger Marcellus
Watkins, Earl Finley
Weaver, Woodrow Wilson
Wilkerson, Jack Roslyn
Wilson, John Edward
Yagemann, William Ferdinand
Zalusky, Bernard

APPENDIX D

PERSONNEL ON THE
SECOND WAR PATROL

3 June to 23 July 1944

Officers

Lt. Cdr. Paul Edward Summers, Commanding Officer

Lt. Cdr. Landon Leslie Davis, Executive Officer

Lt. Cdr. Clifford Charles Grommett, First Lieutenant

Lt. Howard Thomas Fulton, Assistant Engineering Officer

Lt. Mcmillan Houston Johnson, Assistant First Lieutenant

Lt. Ted Nier Swain, Torpedo and Gunnery Officer

Lt(jg). William Lee Bruckart, Communications and Radar Officer

Lt(jg). Francis Michael Fives, Engineering Officer

Lt(jg). John West Red, Jr., Commissary Officer

Ens. Percy Bryan Pike, Electrical Officer

Enlisted

Arcement, Norman John
Attaway, Ralph Winston
Austin, Joseph Charles Cave
Bacskay, Albert Joseph
Bain, Cole Edward
Baron, Leonard
Beaulieu, Laurent
Behney, James Harris
Bennett, Robert
Bouchard, Jacques Florian
Bourgeois, Roger Norman
Bowring, Harry Samuel
Branch, Lamont
Brown, Hubert Nelson
Byrd, Robert
Canty, William Stephen

Carmody, Clarence George

Chapman, Henry Roy

Chinn, Harold

Cordon, Walter Harold

Costello, Irving Francis

Currier, Andrew Louis

Davenport, Bartlett Nathaniel

Depray, Robert Francis

Eberhard, Robert Earl

Eichner, Joseph Frederick

Evans, Jack Jay

Ferguson, Donald Innes

George, Howard Edwin

Grady, William Christopher

Hauptman, Anthony Carl

Herber, Ralph Monroe

Hill, Mervin

Hopper, Gordon Lewis

Ingram, George

Jansen, Kenneth James

Kaup, Norbert Anthony

Kordich, Nickolas

Langin, Lawrence Harold

Large, Bonham Davis

Lederer, Frank Joseph

MacVane, Lloyd Vivian

Madaras, John George

Markham, Clyde Boyd

Martin, Lynn Leonard

McCollum, William Henry

McGuire, Charles Albert, Jr.

Merryman, William Walter

Meyers, Milton Alfred

Michno, Frank Ben

Moffett, George Edward

Morrow, William Franklin, Jr.

Olive, Richard Hugh

O'Neill, John Bernard

Pappas, Paul, Jr.

Parris, Kyle Stanley

Payton, Albert

Richter, Walter Herman

Robinson, Isaac Frederick

Schilling, John Beveridge

Scionti, Santo Sebastian

Smith, Clarence Harrold

Smith, Wendall Tyng, Jr.

Smith, William Clyde

Stimler, Spencer Hunt

Stockslader, Edmund William

Tonkin, Edward Martin

Van Atta, Albert Dillon, Jr.

Walters, Roger Marcellus

Watkins, Earl Finley

Weaver, Woodrow Wilson

Wilkerson, Jack Roslyn

Wilson, John Edward

Yagemann, William Ferdinand

Ylinen, Arthur

Zalusky, Bernard

Appendix E

Personnel on the Third War Patrol

17 August to 28 September 1944

Officers

Cmdr. Paul Edward Summers, Commanding Officer

Lt. Cdr. Landon Leslie Davis, Jr., Executive Officer and Navigator

Lt. Cdr. Clifford Charles Grommet, First Lieutenant

Lt. Howard Thomas Fulton, Assistant Engineering Officer

Lt. McMillan Houston Johnson, Assistant First Lieutenant

Lt. Ted Nier Swain, Torpedo and Gunnery Officer

Lt(jg). Francis Michael Fives, Engineering and Electrical Officer

Lt(jg). John West Red, Jr., Communications Officer

Lt(jg). Richard James Sherlock, Radar Officer

Ens. Charles Kane Bartholomew, Commissary Officer

Enlisted

Arcement, Norman John
Austin, Joseph Charles Cave
Bacskay, Albert Joseph
Bain, Cole Edward
Baron, Leonard
Beaulieu, Laurent
Behney, James Harris
Bennett, Robert
Bixler, Herbert James
Bourgeois, Roger Norman
Bowring, Harry Samuel
Brown, Hubert Nelson
Byrd, Robert

Carmody, Clarence George
Chapman, Henry Roy
Chichak, Andrew Frank
Chinn, Harold
Cordon, Walter Harold
Costello, Irving Francis
Currier, Andrew Louis
Davenport, Bartlett Nathaniel
Demers, Maurice Lawrence
Depray, Robert Francis
Eichner, Joseph Frederick
Elkins, Kelly
Elliot, Allen Charles
Elliot, Richard Eugene
Evans, Jack Jay
Evans, Robert Edward
Ferguson, Donald Innes
Fisk, William Arthur
George, Howard Edwin
Grady, William Christopher
Granum, Peter Anton
Greene, John Herman
Hauptman, Anthony Carl
Hayes, Daniel Edward
Herber, Ralph Monroe
Hill, Mervin
Hopper, Gordon Lewis
Ingram, George
Jansen, Kenneth James
Kaup, Norbert Anthony
Kordich, Nickolas
Lynch, Harry Steven
MacVane, Lloyd Steven

Madaras, John George
Markham, Clyde Boyd
Martin, Lynn Leonard
McGuire, Charles Albert, Jr.
Mendez, Manuel Alfred
Merryman, William Walter
Moffett, George Edward
Morrow, William Franklin, Jr.
Olive, Richard Hugh
Pappas, Paul, Jr.
Parris, Kyle Stanley
Payton, Albert, Jr.
Price, William Francis
Robinson, Isaac Frederick
Schilling, John Beveridge
Smith, Clarence Harold
Smith, Elmer William
Smith, Wendall Tyng, Jr.
Smith, William Clyde
Stimler, Spencer Hunt
Stockslader, Edmund William
Strother, George William
Thompson, Herbert Earl
Tonkin, Edward Martin
Van Atta, Albert Dillon, Jr.
Van Housen, Leroy Ellsworth
Wanerman, Leonard
Weaver, Woodrow Wilson
Wilkerson, Jack Roslyn
Williams, Clarence
Wilson, John Edward
Yagemann, William Ferdinand
Ylinen, Arthur

APPENDIX F

PERSONNEL ON THE FOURTH WAR PATROL

28 October to 30 December 1944

Officers

Capt. Frank Wesley Fenno, Jr., Commanding Officer

Cdr. Earl Twining Hydeman, Prospective Commanding Officer

Lt. Cdr. Landon Leslie Davis, Jr., Executive Officer and Navigator

Lt. Howard Thomas Fulton, Assistant Engineering Officer

Lt. McMillan Houston Johnson, First Lieutenant

Lt. Ted Nier Swain, Torpedo and Gunnery Officer

Lt(jg). Francis Michael Fives, Engineering and Electrical Officer

Lt(jg). John West Red, Jr., Communications Officer

Lt(jg). Richard James Sherlock, Radar Officer

Ens. Charles Kane Bartholomew, Commissary Officer

Enlisted

Arcement, Norman John
Austin, Joseph Charles Cave
Bacskay, Albert Joseph
Beaulieu, Laurent
Behney, James Harris
Bennett, Robert
Bergfeld, Patrick Henry
Bixler, Herman James
Bourgeois, Roger Norman
Bowring, Harry Samuel
Brown, Hubert Nelson
Bulceco, Rufino
Butler, Stanley Freemont
Carmody, Clarence George

Chichak, Andrew Frank
Chinn, Harold
Cordon, Walter Harold
Costello, Irving Francis
Crane, Travis Lee
Currier, Andrew Louis
Davenport, Bartlett Nathaniel
Demers, Maurice Lawrence
Depray, Robert Francis
Elkins, Kelly
Elliot, Allen Charles
Elliot, Richard Eugene
Evans, Robert Edward
Ferguson, Donald Innes
Fisk, William Arthur
Goodson, John Evans
Granum, Peter Anton
Greene, John Herman
Hauptman, Anthony Carl
Hawkins, Ona Denham
Hayes, Daniel Edward
Higgins, Joseph John
Hill, Mervin
Hopper, Gordon Lewis
Ingram, George
Jansen, Kenneth James
Johnson, John Lewis
Kaup, Norbert Anthony
Kordich, Nickolas
Madaras, John George
Madison, Walter Robert
Markham, Clyde Boyd
Martin, Lynn Leonard

McGehee, Ervin Omer
McGuire, Charles Albert, Jr.
Mendez, Manuel Alfred
Merryman, William Walter
Moffett, George Edward
Morrow, William Franklin, Jr.
Noker, Lawrence Edward
Olive, Richard Hugh
Pace, Charles Anthony
Pappas, Paul, Jr.
Parris, Kyle Stanley
Pennell, James Thomas, Jr.
Rechner, George Martin
Redfield, Richard Wentworth
Robinson, Isaac Frederick
Russell, Theodore Kenneth
Smith, Clarence Harrold
Smith, Elmer William
Smith, William Clyde
Stimler, Spencer Hunt
Stockslader, Edmund William
Strother, George William, Jr.
Thompson, Herbert Earl
Tonkin, Edward Martin
Van Atta, Albert Dillon, Jr.
Van Housen, Leroy Ellsworth
Vitello, Donato
Walters, Roger Marcellus
Wanerman, Leonard
Weaver, Woodrow Wilson
Williams, Clarence
Wilson, John Edward
Wood, Paul Jackson
Yagemann, William Ferdinand

Appendix G

Personnel on the Fifth War Patrol

23 January to 12 February 1945

Officers

Cdr. Paul Edward Summers, Commanding Officer

Lt. Cdr. William Jack Bush, Prospective Commanding Officer

Lt. Cdr. Lynn Stanley Orser, Executive Officer

Lt. McMillan Houston Johnson, First Lieutenant

Lt. Ted Nier Swain, Torpedo and Gunnery Officer

Lt. Francis Michael Fives, Engineering and Electrical Officer

Lt(jg). John West Red, Jr., Communications Officer

Lt(jg). Richard James Sherlock, Radar Officer

Lt(jg). Charles Kane Bartholomew, Commissary Officer

Ens. Edmund Eugene De Paul, Assistant Engineering Officer

Enlisted

Arcement, Norman John
Austin, Joseph Charles Cave
Bacskay, Albert Joseph
Beaulieu, Laurent
Behney, James Harris
Bennett, Robert
Berganio, Fermin Roquero
Bergfeld, Patrick Henry
Bixler, Herbert James
Bourgeois, Roger Norman
Bowring, Harry Samuel
Butler, Stanley Freemont
Carmody, Clarence George
Chichak, Andrew Frank
Cordon, Walter Harold
Crane, Travis Lee

Currier, Andrew Louis
Davenport, Bartlett Nathaniel
Demers, Maurice Lawrence
Elkins, Kelly
Elliot, Allen Charles
Elliot, Richard Eugene
Evans, Robert Edward
Fisk, William Arthur
Goodson, John Evans
Granum, Peter Anton
Greene, John Herman
Hawkins, Ona Denham
Hayes, Daniel Edward
Higgins, Joseph John
Hill, Mervin
Hopper, Gordon Lewis
Ingram, George
Jansen, Kenneth James
Johnson, John Lewis
Kapustynski, John
Kordich, Nickolas
Madaras, John George
Madison, Walter Robert
Martin, Lynn Leonard
McGehee, Ervin Omer
McGrath, James Walter
McGuire, Charles Albert, Jr.
Mendez, Manuel Alfred
Merryman, William Walter
Moffett, George Edward
Morrow, William Franklin, Jr.
Noker, Lawrence Edward

Osstander, Glenn
Pace, Charles Anthony
Pappas, Paul, Jr.
Parris, Kyle Stanley
Pennell, James Thomas, Jr.
Rechner, George Martin
Redfield, Richard Wentworth
Rice, Charles McClellen
Russell, Theodore Kenneth
Schwartz, Ernest Edward
Shepard, Calvin Kay
Smith, Addison Russell
Smith, Clarence Harrold
Smith, Elmer William
Smith, Jess "D", Jr.
Smith, William Clyde
Stimler, Spencer Hunt
Stockslader, Edmund William
Strother, George William
Tansil, Jack Spencer
Thompson, Herbert Earl
Tonkin, Edward Martin
Van Housen, Leroy Ellsworth
Vitello, Donato
Wagner, Edmond Follmer
Walters, Roger Marcellus
Wanerman, Leonard
Weaver, Woodrow Wilson
Whitt, Lloyd Arthur
Williams, Clarence
Wilson, John Edward
Yagemann, William Ferdinand

Appendix H

Personnel on the Sixth War Patrol

25 February to 24 April 1945

Officers

Cdr. Paul Edward Summers, Commanding Officer

Lt Cdr. William Jack Bush, Prospective Commanding Officer

Lt. Cdr. Lynn Stanley Orser, Executive Officer and Navigator

Lt. McMillan Houston Johnson, First Lieutenant

Lt. Ted Nier Swain, Torpedo and Gunnery Officer

Lt. Francis Michael Fives, Engineering and Electrical Officer

Lt(jg). John West Red, Jr., Communications Officer

Lt(jg). Richard James Sherlock, Radar Officer

Lt(jg). Charles Kane Bartholomew, Commissary Officer

Enlisted

Aiken, William Ives
Arcement, Norman John
Austin, Joseph Charles Cave
Bacskay, Albert Joseph
Beaulieu, Laurent
Behney, James Harris
Bennett, Robert
Berganio, Fermin Roquero
Bergfeld, Patrick Henry
Bixler, Herbert James
Bourgeois, Roger Norman
Bowring, Harry Samuel
Butler, Stanley Freemont
Carmody, Clarence George
Chichak, Andrew Frank

Cordon, Walter Harold
Crane, Travis Lee
Currier, Andrew Louis
Davenport, Bartlett Nathaniel
De Lorme, Murray Neil
Demers, Maurice Lawrence
Elkins, Kelly
Elliot, Allen Charles
Elliot, Richard Eugene
Evans, Robert Edward
Fisk, William Arthur
Goodson, John Evans
Granum, Peter Anton
Greene, John Herman
Hawkins, Ona Denham
Hayes, Daniel Edward
Higgins, Joseph John
Hill, Mervin
Hopper, Gordon Lewis
Ingram, George
Jansen, Kenneth James
Johnson, John Lewis
Kordich, Nickolas
Madaras, John George
Madison, Walter Robert
Martin, Lynn Leonard
McGehee, Ervin Omer
McGrath, James Walter
McGuire, Charles Albert, Jr.
Mendez, Manuel Alfred
Merryman, William Walter
Moffett, George Edward
Morrow, William Franklin, Jr.

Mountan, Andrew Wray
Noker, Lawrence Edward
Osstander, Glenn
Pace, Charles Anthony
Pappas, Paul, Jr.
Pennell, James Thomas, Jr.
Rechner, George Martin
Redfield, Richard Wentworth
Rice, Charles Mc Clellen
Russell, Theodore Kenneth
Schwartz, Ernest Edward
Sheehan, Thomas Francis
Shepard, Calvin Kay
Smith, Addison Russell
Smith, Clarence Harrold
Smith, Elmer William
Smith, Jess "D", Jr.
Smith, William Clyde
Stimler, Spencer Hunt
Stockslader, Edmund William
Stoll, Robert, Jr.
Strother, George William, Jr.
Tansil, Jack Spencer
Thompson, Herbert Earl
Tonkin, Edward Martin
Van Housen, Leroy Ellsworth
Vitello, Donato
Wagner, Edmond Follmer
Walters, Roger Marcellus
Wanerman, Leonard
Weaver, Woodrow Wilson
Williams, Clarence
Wilson, John Edward
Yagemann, William Ferdinand

APPENDIX I

POWs Rescued By *PAMPANITO*

September 15, 1944

Australians

Boulter, James L.
Browne, J. F. M.
Bullock, Reginald C.
Chivars, H.C.
Cocking, A. John
Coombes, Frank J.
Comford, Roydon C.
Cunneen, D. William
Curran, M. W.
Farlow, Cliff L.
Farmer, Frank E.
Farrands, M. Robert
Flynn, David A.
Gainger, R. J.
Gollin, Reg. Glen
Harris, Reginald J.
Hart, Reginald H.
Hocking, John R.
Holcroft, Frank
Jesse, Frank W.
Kinleyside, Harry L.
Lansdowne, James H.
Latham, C.T.S.

Longey, Claude
Lynch, Darcy F.
Madden, Charles W.
Martin, Harold D.
Mawby, Raymond H.
McArdle, Donald F.
McKechnie, Charles B.
McKittrick, William H.
Miscamble, Ronald C.
Pascoe, T. A.
Pickett, Harry
Renton, K.C.
Smith, C. F.
Smith, C. G.
Smith, Pat
Stewart, Reginald S.
Turner, Jack W.
Vickers, J. A.
Wall, Robert J.
Weigand, Hilton G.
White, Strachan M.
Williams, Ken
Winter, Alfred D.
Winter, Walter V.

British

Anderson, C.
Baldwin, G.
Barker, H. J.
Brierley, Thomas B.
Campbell, John *
Costello, Stanley
Cray, William
Cresswell, Douglas A.
Everitt, W.
Fieldhouse, Ernest
Harrison, Jesse
Hughes, Ernest
Jay, C.

Jones, Harry
Kidman, W.
Mandley, William A.
Nobbs, A.
Ogden, Alfred
Perry, Charles A.
Smethurst, Harry
Smith, Denny
Smith, Thomas
Taylor, Thomas
Ward, George K.
Whiley, Samuel T.
Wiles, F .E.

* Deceased immediately following rescue

Appendix J

Pampanito Staff and Volunteers 2000

Jim Adams
Dominic Alleluia
Chris Bach
Marilyn Bagshaw
Kathleen Balauat
Al Burnham
Richard Carbine
David Cerejo
Chris Edwards
Bob Fajardo
Eleanor Fajardo
Dennis Franklin
Harold Franklin
Ted Hamiter
Waldon Hom
Tom Horsfall
Carye Johnson
Michael Lannon
Terry Lindell
Al McDonald
Carlos Miller

Harry Nystrom
Kevin O'Flaherty
Bill Oliver
John Paulin
Rich Pekelney
Jim Pelmulder
Danilo Prado
Tom Richardson
Aldona Sendzikas
Joe Senft
Harold Strunk
Bob Taylor
Richard Thomas
John Tomko
Michael Toussand
Len Vaden
Aaron Washington
Lee Williams
Marvin Wong
Ray Yuann

Appendix K

Sponsors

Individuals and Organizations

Abrams, Arnie
Adams, Jim
Anderson, Scott
Arco Petroleum Products Company
August Link - Surcom Associates, Inc.
Bansemer, Henry
Bartowski, Steve
Beeler, Jim
Brown, Duncan
Bugner, Rick
C&D Equipment Co., Dick Pecor
Coats, Roy
Crowley Maritime
Devoe (Ameron) Paint Company
Diffily, Jack
Doll, Bill
Donzelli, William
Downs, Robert
DuVall, Dennis
Eichner, Joseph
Engstrom, Henry
Fedlund, George
Ferrigan, James
Field, Pecos Bill
Finelli, Steve
Fishfader, Stanley
Godeck, Larry
Granum, Mrs. Peter
Greene, John
Gyro Systems Inc., Buddy Creakmore
Hanz, Mike
Harris, Lowell
Hauck, Dave
Hill, Mervin
Hopper Gordon
Horsfall, Tom
Hubble Electric Heater Company
Huselid, Jeff
Instruments East
Jackson, Charles E.
Jones, Al
Jones, Dave
Junkin, Johne
Kasper, Darryl
Kelly, Dennis
Kollmorgan Electro-Optics

Krasner, Eric H.
Lehman, Ted
Lenox, Andy
Lindel, Terry
Manning, Charles
Manson Crane - Glenn Edwards
    and Pete Paup
McDonald, Ann A.
McDonald, Brian
McGrahan, Jim
Merz, Don
Mitz, Andrew
Morgan, Tom
Nash Engineering
Nelson, Chuck
Paine, Dr. T.O.
Pekelney, Richard
Phillips, Charles
Proc, Jerry
Risser, Ruby
Raudso, Robert
Russell, David
Scale Effects - Ed Williams
Scherer, Donald
Schick, H. Alton
Schoonmaker
Sea River Corporation
Senft, Joe
Smith Clock Co., - David Smith
Smith, Hugh
Snider, Tony
Soldering, Dean
Stanford Submersible Research
    Project - Scott Anderson, Mark
    Brius, Scott Chamness, Tony
    Stone
Stinson, Dave
Tara, Mike
Taylor, Doc
Thekan, Paul

Thorpe, Ed
Unitek Environmental Services,
    Inc.
Vaden, Len
Van Lennep, William
Vaughan, Allan
Weaver, Woodrow Wilson
Wittenborn, Charles
Wright, Jack

Non-Profit Museums

Historical Electronics Museum Inc.
HMS *Haida*
USS *Bowfin*
USS *Cobia*
USS *Cod*
USS *Croaker*
USS *Kidd*, Louisiana Naval War
    Memorial Commission
USS *Lionfish*
USS *Requin*
USS *Silversides*
USS *Torsk*

U.S. Government Agencies

Port of Richmond California
U.S. Maritime Administration,
    Suisun Bay Reserve Fleet
U.S. Naval Historical Center
U.S. Naval Inactive Ships, Pearl
    Harbor
U.S. Navy Naval Security Group
U.S. National Security Agency
U.S. National Archives, Pacific Si-
    erra Region
U.S. National Park Service, San
    Francisco National Maritime
    National Historical Park

BIBLIOGRAPHY

Batchelor, John, Louis S. Casey and Antony Preston. *Sea Power, A Modern Illustrated Military History.* London: Phoebus Publishing Company, 1979.

"BCDC approves sub at Pier 45." *San Francisco Examiner,* Nov. 21, 1975.

Booth, Russell. "USS *Pampanito:* The Last Three War Patrols." *Sea Letter.* National Maritime Museum Association, Spring 1987.

Buckley, Dan. "Submarine fights its way back to top." *Sacramento Union,* June 7, 1981,

Chesneau, Roger, Ed. *Conway's All the World's Fighting Ships 1922-1946.* London: Conway Maritime Press, 1980.

Dictionary of American Naval Fighting Ships. Vol. V. Washington: Naval History Division, 1970

Francis, T.L. *Submarines, Leviathans of the Deep.* New York: MetroBooks, 1997.

Glover, Malcolm. "WW II sub to be berthed at the wharf." *San Francisco Examiner.* May 28, 1981.

Houghteling, Joseph C. "The Quest for the *Pampanito*: A New Association Direction." *Sea Letter.* The National Maritime Museum Association, Winter 1999.

Kimmett, Larry and Margaret Regis. *U.S. Submarines in World War II, An Illustrated History.* Seattle, Washington: Navigator Publishing, 1996.

Kusserow, H.W. "Available to S.F. Role for a sub: Tourist display." *San Francisco Examiner.* May 9, 1974.

--   "WWII sub sought as tourist display." *San Francisco Examiner.* May 9, 1974.

Ludlow, Lynn. "Pampanito file: Documents revive harsh memory of war." *San Francisco Sunday Examiner & Chronicle.* July 18, 1976

--   "Sub, dogged by tragedy, still seeking berth here." --   --

Michno, Gregory F. *USS Pampanito, Killer-Angel.* Norman, Oklahoma: University of Oklahoma Press, 2000.

Mueller, William B. *"Pampanito." Sea Classics.* Challenge Publications, Inc. January, 1978.

Navigation Dictionary. Washington: U.S. Government Printing Office, 1969.

Nolte, Carl. "Plan to Display Submarine at Wharf Gets OK." *San Francisco Chronicle.* May 29, 1981.

Padfield, Peter. *War Beneath the Sea.* New York: John Wiley & Sons, Inc., 1995.

Roscoe, Theodore. *United States Submarine Operations in World War II.* Annapolis, Maryland: Naval Institute Press, 1949.

Smith, Barry D. "U.S.S. *Pampanito." Sea Classics.* Challenge Publications, Inc. January/February, 1987.

Sumrall, Robert F. *USS Bowfin (SS-287).* Missoula, Montana: Pictorial Histories Publishing Company, 1999.

Thomas, William G. "A True and Faithful Account of How San Francisco Maritime National Historical Park was Created." *Sea Letter.* The National Maritime Museum Association. Winter, 1999.

Whitwell, Les. "USS *Pampanito* floats history all its own." *Tahoe Tribune.* Sept. 24, 1982.

Wilson, Leon. "The Jungle Ordeal of Allied POWs." *San Francisco Sunday Examiner & Chronicle.* Sept. 16, 1979.

Wong, Ken. "Sub makes debut as museum; Memorial submarine now berthed here at Pier 45." *San Francisco Examiner*, Mar. 16, 1982.

ABOUT THE AUTHOR

Capt. Jaffee graduated from the U.S. Merchant Marine Academy at Kings Point, New York. He sailed as a licensed deck officer, receiving his master's papers at the age of twenty-six. Traveling the oceans many times, he has visited just about every country that touches water. He was at one time involved in sportfishing and was a pioneer in whalewatching in Northern California. He earned a master's degree in Public Administration from California State University at Hayward.

Formerly employed by the Maritime Administration as Superintendent of the Suisun Bay Reserve Fleet, he has taught as an adjunct professor at the California Maritime Academy and was first officer on the SS *Jeremiah O'Brien* during her epic return to Europe for the 50th Anniversary of D-Day in 1994.

Index

203